D1083830

Great Advertising Campaigns

Great
Advertising
Campaigns

GOALS

AND

ACCOMPLISHMENTS

Nicholas Ind

NTC Business Books

a division of *NTC Publishing Group* • Lincolnwood, Illinois USA

CONTENTS

ACKNOWLEDGEMENTS

Inevitably, in writing a series of case studies one is dependent on the support and co-operation of a large number of people. Without their input, there would be no book. In particular I would like to thank:

Jan Boyle, Alyson Henning and Mike Lotito of Ammirati & Puris in New York; Scott Diel, Geoff Hayes, Peter Lubalin and Scott Kellegher of TBWA in New York; Maryanne O' Brien, Harish Bhandari, Bill Miller, Mark Johnson and Peter Engel of Fallon McElligott in Minneapolis; Chris Riley and Mark Barden of Weiden & Kennedy in Portland, Oregon; Knut Andresen of New Deal in Oslo; Peter Gilson of CLM/BBDO in Paris; Sammy Harari and Paul Nathan of Harari Page in London; Romola Christopherson at the Department of Health in London; Maggie Taylor, Adrian Kemsley and Paul Cowan of Cowan, Kemsley, Taylor in London; Mike Willis and Phil Adams of Bartle Bogle Hegarty in London; Sarah Carter and Alan Ayres of BMP DDB Needham in London; Anne MacCaig of Lever Brothers in London; Fiona Inkley, Sam Carter and Mike Chick of JWT in London; Richard Block, once of Publicis and now of JWT in London. Also my editor at Kogan Page, Philip Mudd, for directing my efforts; and my wife, Vivi, for her suggestions and criticisms.

PREFACE

The idea for a case book of advertising campaigns came from the thought that the creation and development of advertising is not only interesting in its own right, but also insightful into how advertising works. There are, of course, already many books which explore the theory of advertising and there are indeed books of case histories, albeit mostly research and analytically based. *Great Advertising Campaigns* is neither of these. The cases do include the results of a campaign and they do include some theory, but the primary focus is on *the process of campaign creation*. Although I have tried to draw the strands of each case together, the reader can draw his or her own conclusions about whether a campaign is great or not.

As regards the choice of campaigns to be labelled 'great', the facts are as follows. First, some campaigns are genuinely 'great', by which I mean that they stand head and shoulders above the mass of advertising; that they are inspired, unique pieces of creativity. Others are probably only good, clever pieces of advertising, which have met their objectives, without extending the idea of what advertising can do. Yet others are too new to be judged. Second, having once reviewed a book of case histories, which I found boring because each case made the same points, I have sought variety in both choice and approach. Inevitably, there are some common themes, but I believe this is because brands face common opportunities and threats. Finally, the choice is eclectic, and is based on my idea of what works from both a business and creative perspective. There are other campaigns which would work equally well, but either client sensitivity to the release of information or the need for balance prevented them being included.

The research process for the book consisted of an initial phase of desk research, followed up by one-to-one interviews with those involved in the process of creating the individual campaigns. The interviews were conducted in the UK, USA, Norway and France during 1991 and 1992.

Inevitably, with a book involving contemporary issues, things rapidly go out of date, but within reason I have updated the cases up until the last minute before publication. What I hope will not go out of date is the perceived quality of the campaigns featured in this book.

Nicholas Ind
November 1992

INTRODUCTION

Whereas the reader will most likely scan the introduction before launching into this book, it has actually been written last. It may be that writers always finish with the introduction, but I mention it here in order to make a specific point. I started the book relatively free of preconceptions about the general points the cases would make. There was no hidden agenda of trying to prove, for example, that great advertising only comes from in-depth research or even from ignoring research — although there do seem to be a number of cases of the latter. The stories of each campaign provide their own insights. All I will attempt with the introduction, therefore, is to set out what seem to be, with hindsight, the common themes of the book.

DON'T ACCEPT THE ACCEPTED WISDOM

Over time, certain advertising conventions become sufficiently well established to become guiding principles for most advertisers and their agencies. One of them used to be that you can't use humour to sell financial services, until Barclays Bank and the Leeds Permanent Building Society proved you could. Similarly, in the US, spirits advertising used to concentrate on associating a brand with sexy images, until Absolut Vodka (chapter 1) came along and simply showed a beautifully photographed bottle with a witty headline. Also, the imagery of jeans advertising had been consistently focused on style images until Lee jeans built a campaign based on a fit message (chapter 10).

Conventional wisdom would also suggest that the brand needs to be featured prominently in the advertising. Yet Bartle Bogle Hegarty have produced advertising for Phileas Fogg snacks where the product is not seen (chapter 13) and Weiden & Kennedy have produced work for Nike (chapter 12) where the communication is about fitness or style or an approach to life rather than sports shoes.

What these advertisers have in common is the confidence to challenge and question. Perhaps that is not surprising, given that brands such as Nike, Phileas Fogg and Absolut Vodka were launched into highly competitive markets, where playing by the rules would have ensured a status of also-rans. The benefit to each of these advertisers in creating their own framework is that their advertising (and the brand) gets noticed as being distinctive and different.

CAUTION: RESEARCH, HANDLE WITH CARE

One of the core beliefs of the advertising industry is that consumer research produces better advertising. Certainly, the focus on planning and research has helped to move the image of the industry away from being superficial towards being more professional and analytical. However, has research helped advertising creativity and effectiveness? The best that can be said is sometimes. Absolut ignored the results of research that said the brand would never work. Phileas Fogg ignored research that said their packs should have windows. In contrast, the advertising for Solid Fuel (chapter 5) and Barclaycard (chapter 11) was created from the results of qualitative research. When to ignore and when to accept the findings of research is a delicate judgement. I am sure that there are many examples of advertisers who ignore research and live to rue the day, just as there are famous examples of those who ignored research and succeeded.

The lesson that perhaps should be learnt from this is that research has limitations and should be an aid to judgement, rather than an alternative to it. The great campaigns in this book mostly used research to acquire an understanding of consumer perspectives before the process of creating ads. They did not use research to check whether individual ads communicated what they set out to do. If they did, I am sure that many of the ads in this book would never have run. The best advertising (as noted above), challenges the conventions. Research is generally unable to provide an accurate picture of the likely effectiveness of advertising that ignores the norms. What it can do, if used creatively, is provide the insight to enable that advertising to be produced in the first place.

DON'T TAKE YOURSELF TOO SERIOUSLY

Not surprisingly, advertisers and their agencies take their brands seriously. A marketing director and an account director will spend much of their daily lives talking about and thinking about a brand and how to communicate its values. The danger in this is that you start to think that the brand assumes the same sort of importance in the consumer's life. However, most brands are relatively inconsequential purchases and therefore do not occupy much of a consumer's thinking time. Rather than trying to overstate a brand's importance, there seems to be much more credibility if a self-deprecating attitude is taken. Persil Washing-Up Liquid (chapter 3) exemplifies this approach, especially when contrasted with Procter and Gamble; as do Oslo Public Transport (chapter 2), Nike (chapter 12) and Phileas Fogg (chapter 13). All these advertisers are prepared to take risks and are prepared to laugh at themselves. It not only seems more credible, it also seems to create a more emotional response to the advertising.

BUILDING A BRAND TAKES TIME

Most of the cases in this book are of campaigns which have run over a number of years. That is not to say they slavishly follow an idea, come what may. Some of the advertisers have changed their strategy or refocused it. BMW (chapter 9), for example, found that its original strategy was becoming out-dated because of consumer attitudes and the new competition from Japan. They reworked their advertising strategy to make it relevant. Similarly, Absolut Vodka adapted the rules it had set for itself, because it found the original definition of the creative approach too limiting. Although Apple Computers (chapter 14) advertising all looks different, there is a common campaign theme based on empowerment.

The benefit of this consistency of approach is that it achieves economies of scale. Apple could launch their Powerbook computer three years after the competition and still take 25 per cent of the European portable computer market, because they had a long-established and clearly defined brand image (and a great product). The consistency also helps to create an emotional link between an advertiser and its consumers. Some commentators would argue that as consumers become more sophisticated and advertising literate, communications need to stress rational rather than emotional reasons for buying a product or service. I would have no argument with the importance of rational buying triggers. However, I would also argue that taking into account the speed with which companies are able to duplicate each other's product performance and the consequent difficulty of differentiation, the emotional, non-rational factors for buying a product or service are even more important. It is also the area where advertising can be most influential.

INTERNATIONAL ADVERTISING

The advertising industry has long argued about the relative benefits of international advertising. Its critics argue that it creates a blandness, even if there are benefits to be derived from creating a global corporate or brand image. Although there are international campaigns in this book, I do not believe any of them are bland. This is because, with the exception of Apple Computers, all the campaigns which became international did so inadvertently. The American campaigns for Nike and Absolut Vodka were introduced into Europe because they had worked so well for the indigenous market for which they were created.

Much of the debate about the quality of international advertising revolves around the homogeneity or heterogeneity of consumers in different countries. The cultural factor is undoubtedly important. However, I believe the real reason for bland international advertising is the difficulty of administering the process. Impose a campaign from the centre and you create ill will and arguments about the appropriateness of the work to the local market. Involve local markets in the process and compromises will be made in the creative development and its application. Neither route results in good work. What does is a strong advertising idea, which works so well in its local market that other countries want to buy into the strategy and/or the execution.

1

ABSOLUT VODKA IN THE US

ABSOLUT PERFECTION

THE PRINT CAMPAIGN OF THE 1980s

In 1980 Absolut Vodka was a tiny brand selling 12,000 cases a year in the US. By 1991 Absolut was the market leader of the imported vodka sector, with sales of 2.7 million cases. This massive increase has been achieved not by price, (Absolut is a premium positioned product), nor by availability (Absolut is very much an urban brand), but by advertising. Advertising has given a desirable personality to a colourless, tasteless and virtually odourless product, which is nearly always consumed with a mixer. Even if some claim to be able to tell the difference between one vodka and another — at least in the quality of hangover — consumers buy Absolut in preference to other vodkas not because of taste, but because of what it says about them. What Absolut advertising has done is to create a seemingly enduring fashion for a product which research said had very little going for it.

Background

In the mind of the American consumer, Vodka was associated with Russia. The brand leader of the imported sector in 1980 was Russian: Stolichnaya, and even the domestically produced brands sported Russian names: Smirnoff, Popov, Kamchatka. In contrast, Absolut was Swedish and American associations with Sweden were Volvo cars and hot tubs. To check the viability of the brand, Michel Roux, who was President of Carillon (Absolut's importer), decided to invest $65,000 on a market research study. This confirmed everyone's worst fears. The name was seen as too gimmicky, the bottle shape was ugly and bartenders found it hard to pour, the shelf prominence was limited and of course there was no credibility for a vodka brand made in Sweden. The market researcher's recommendation was to drop the product. However, Roux decided to ignore this advice. His view was that the product was so different from consumer's notions of what a vodka should be that market research could not get a reading on it. In any case, what was needed was some strong advertising to help give the brand a personality.

THE SEARCH FOR ABSOLUT PERFECTION

One of the agencies pitching for the Absolut account was TBWA in New York. They realised that although vodka was essentially a commodity product, it was important that the quality of the product 'with its 400 years of Swedish tradition' was communicated. However, quality by itself would not be enough. To justify its premium price, Absolut had to become fashionable — to be the drink people wanted to be seen drinking. The initial approach to creating awareness and fashionability for the brand was to try and build on the Swedish heritage of the product. Rather than ignoring what might be a disadvantage, ideas were developed depicting Swedes in hot tubs and similar Swedish settings.

The ads fitted in well with other US liquor campaigns which favoured lifestyle images, preferably with sexy women, as a way of attracting attention. However, Geoff Hayes, who was a newly hired Art Director from Britain, felt that there was something missing. It was all too predictable; and there was nothing that suggested the product was a premium brand. For the brand to succeed, it had to break the conventions of liquor advertising, not follow them. Rather than using Swedishness to create the brand personality, why not use the quirkiness of the name and the bottle shape to communicate quality and fashion? Three days before the presentation to Carillon, Geoff Hayes came up with the solution:

> I was sitting watching TV and drawing the bottle and I remember drawing a halo over its top and adding a line something like 'It's absolutely perfect'. I came in the next morning and showed it to Graham, my writer, who said you don't have to say that, just say 'Absolut Perfection'. And suddenly we thought we had something. The thing that made

us think it was a campaign was that in five minutes we had ten ideas.

The concepts for the pitch all featured the strange-shaped bottle as the hero, to which was added a two-word line always starting with 'Absolut' and finishing with a quality word such as 'Perfection' or 'Clarity' (Figure 1). There was no need to tell any product story because that was etched on to the bottle itself. The quirkiness of the product was accurately reflected by the quirkiness of the advertising. Making the bottle the hero was likely to appeal to the client, but it was the wit and whimsy of the headline in conjunction with the visual that gave the ads their charm and sophistication. Although Michel Roux was presented with a variety of campaign approaches, including the Swedish hot tub, everyone felt there was going to be only one winner: Roux was charmed by 'Absolut Perfection' and TBWA were awarded the business.

MAKING THE IDEA WORK

What TBWA had created was an advertising idea that provided a point of difference from other brands in the market. The advertising idea also aimed to put Absolut on a pedestal and make it a symbol of success and sophistication. If the idea could be converted into reality, Michel Roux thought that one day Absolut might match Stolichnaya's sales. However, there was no fast way of building awareness and desirability (or so everyone thought), because in the US spirits advertisers cannot use television or radio. Therefore TBWA had to think in terms of magazines, billboards and bus shelters.

TBWA's reaction to the media limitation was to try to achieve the same level of production values that would normally be found in TV films. If the bottle was to be the hero, it needed to be shot perfectly; it needed to be sensual and appealing and to have impact on the page. Realising that the execution of the concept was key to its success, Geoff Hayes found a photographer called Steve Bronstein who understood his idea of shooting the bottle so that its texture and shape were dominant. In the first three years of the campaign, TBWA produced just six ads (in the last three they have produced 55). All of the ideas were perfectly crafted, concentrated on quality messages and were compelling in the simplicity of the

Figure 1 Absolut Perfection

idea and their execution. They could also be frighteningly expensive to produce. One of the later, more complex ideas was rumoured to have cost $40,000. Nor were Carillon frightened of spending media money to support the brand; Roux recognised that the brand's added value came from the image created by advertising.

Consequently, Absolut outspent both domestic and imported competition in terms of advertising per case. In 1982, for example, Absolut were spending $10.69 per case compared with $3.09 for Stolichnaya, $8.68 for Finlandia and $1.08 for Smirnoff. When the creative superiority of the Absolut campaign is taken into account, it is perhaps not surprising that in 1983 Absolut matched Finlandia's sales of 160,000 cases. Stolichnaya were still a long way ahead with 450,000 cases, but Absolut were catching up. The advertising had undoubted appeal to consumers' sense of humour and intellect. People were asking for Absolut by name in bars, even when they were drinking Bloody Marys and totally unable to taste the vodka itself. Buying Absolut was making a statement that you could afford to pay that little bit extra for superior quality. Michel Roux says:

> The US is a country of aspirations. People want to have a better life. Vodka has the same qualities as fine cognac. Of course it takes longer to make a fine cognac, but the quality of craftsmanship is the same. That craftsmanship and the image we project give consumers self confidence. They feel comfortable with the product; they feel good looking at it and they feel good consuming it.[1]

EXTENDING PERFECTION

> Because the idea is so simple, you have to do different things; do the unexpected. Otherwise people would get tired of the campaign very quickly.[2]

Having seen the positive results of the initial phase of the campaign, Carillon upped the total advertising spend significantly in the mid-1980s. However, the increased media presence also created the possibility of over-exposure of some of the ads. To overcome this, the number of ads produced was increased: five in

1985, six in 1986 and eleven in 1987. This in turn created a problem in finding enough 'quality' themes. Eventually, Absolut's advertising rules had to be rewritten. Nothing would be done to undermine the premium positioning of the brand, but intriguingly sophisticated ads would now be mixed in with the more quality based themes. The success of this approach can be attributed to two key factors. First, although the rules were being changed, the tone and style of the campaign remained the same: these were still identifiably Absolut ads. Second, within the campaign idea, both Michel Roux and TBWA recognised the importance of innovation; of not being a slave to something unsustainable; and of finding new ideas that would advance Absolut's position as a fashionable, sophisticated product. It is this balance of continuity and freshness that has kept the campaign alive.

The first real break with tradition was the move away from a photographic presentation of the bottle. Michel Roux came up with the idea of getting an artist to paint the Absolut bottle. If the right artist could be found, this would suggest that Absolut was at the forefront of contemporary culture. As a sophisticated brand that set trends, there could be only one choice: Andy Warhol. Not only had he once been a commercial artist, but he had also transformed Campbell's Soup tins into a cultural icon and was now America's highest profile and most fashionable artist. Although both Roux's own staff and the agency were unsure about the idea, Roux went ahead and commissioned Warhol. The result was a powerful illustration with the brand name writ large and captioned 'Absolut Warhol'. Not surprisingly, the Warhol ad achieved the desired effect and spawned a series of artist paintings: Absolut Haring (1986) (Figure 2), Absolut Scharf (1987) and Absolut Britto (1990) being among the better known.

The artist series also led Roux and TBWA to cast around and look at other brand associations which might be useful in developing the fashionable status of the brand. One of the obvious solutions was to use fashion designers. This would tie in perfectly with the image-driven target market for Absolut who would aspire to designer name clothes. A ten-page insert aimed at females was developed, entitled 'Absolut Fashion'. In this instance the bottle itself did not appear, rather parts or the whole of the bottle were woven into the dress design or printed on to stockings. The concept was then extended into an eight-page menswear insert

Figure 2 Absolut Haring

Figure 3 Absolut Centrefold

Figure 4 Absolut L.A.

Figure 5 Absolut Chicago

Figure 6 Absolut Peppar

be aware of all stories that are about to run in his ... "We're from the Ramsey Review. It's another news-
newspaper. You might even go so far as to say the ... he was still baffled. Walter repeated the name,
lisher, if not aware of the stories before th ... me very carefully, ensuring that she under-
at least read the stories once they come ... and every syllable. She looked at us quizzi-
they tell you is standard operating proc ... suddenly she smiled.
nalism school anyway. But, in a situation like ... es," she pointed to the grey lumps on her drive-
Larry and Sid's full attention was required ... Ramzee Reyou, si, si, gee Ramzee Reyou."
a very volatile account roster, such attention ... oned for us to come in. We sat down in her
dered frivolous if not out of the question e ... he was very hospitable. She offered us coffee,
Naturally, Larry was oblivious to the ... es, and cake. Walter was insistent we get the
must admit he took the news with rela ...
don't even think that bearing my sto ... ma'am. Just the facts." Walter asked the
from calling the Sheriff. I really did ... and she gave her answers in a tongue
led the mess he was in. I was in fo ... er heard before.

As we pulled into the d ... me foo no work." Translation: the
spread-eagle under a willow ... broken down.
was rather warm and humi ... nom Brooky." She took her car
let him in for the night. We ... Ford.
that, so he managed to find hi ... gh wich eeem." The car stayed
peaceful spot on the proper ...
know that even though we ha ... k's lot.
for the night, he wasn't about ... gee engeen goo bu gee casseet

CHAPTER ... ed up her car the next day, the
... but her cassette radio had
On Friday morning, Walte ... en.
close to looking, and perhaps ... seet. Casseet fro o cas oh so
live newspaper men. We boldly ... place nobodee casseet. He say
armed with notepad, pencils ... esponseeble." Brook wouldn't
camera. Welcome to the glamor ... er, claiming that his entire lot
tigative journalism. ... at night and that it would be
We were following a "hot ... rything that had been stolen.
been a rash of car radio thefts ... hew nom." I don't know what
had just heard about a woma ...
information. He was especially ... ell me new casseet. Gee as ho.
so we jumped into his speedy ... had offered to sell her a new
to run every stop sign and re ... declined and threatened to call
I discovered just a block ... us she did.
that I had neglected to bring ... y-five minutes to get her story.
tantrum, and in this reporter ... ust trying to understand what
reacted quite unnecessarily ... worth the trouble. The story it-
had to stop at several drug ... ven though we were unsure if it
a roll of black-and-white fil ... rall county-wide increase in car
his life that while the two ...
time looking for film, a repo ... ttractive woman and I really
had already interviewed the w ... e coffee and cake but Walter
in to his editor. ... me pictures and say goodbye.
As we finally drove up ...
what appeared to be sever ... TER EIGHT
surmised could only have be ...
view. It was an ominous sign ... but, but this time I was careful
dropped my camera on the pav ... d barge right in as usual. I knew
ominous sign. ... I really didn't want him to have
We rang the doorbell and with ... nocked softly. If I were to knock
impeccably dressed, middle-aged French wo ... brother's door it would certainly
the door. We introduced ourselves as the reporter and ... used suspicion.
photographer from the Ramsey Review.
"Jour no from de Ramzee Recaw?" ... "It's me, Dan. Can I come in?" I waited several sec-
Walter and I looked at each other. It was the third and ... onds for a reply but there was none, so I decided to open
most ominous sign yet. ... the door. Larry was alone and on the phone. I sat down
"We're from the Ramsey Review," said Walter. She ... in front of him and waited patiently for him to get off.
looked at us like we were from a different galaxy. ... "Are you on hold?" I asked after several minutes had
passed without either of us saying a word. He nodded
affirmatively. He seemed a little agitated at my question

ABSOLUT PEPPAR

IMPORTED

and then into a product design insert featuring tables and chairs in the shape of Absolut bottles.

Once released from the constraint of specific quality messages, the visual and verbal inventiveness of the campaign took off. Ads were produced for specific media, so that Absolut Centrefold (Figure 3) in *Playboy* magazine featured a naked bottle, while Absolut Split in the *Wall Street Journal* featured half a bottle on either side of the stock listings. Ads were produced for specific occasions, such as a Christmas special called Absolut Wonderland, which featured a bottle encased in a liquid film with imitation snow — a two-dimensional version of the sort of glass snow globe used in *Citizen Kane*. This particular idea was so distinctive that it generated an estimated $10 million in free print and TV coverage in both local and network news shows.

A whole series of ads was produced featuring the bottle as locations. The Absolut bottle was Central Park in Absolut Manhattan, a swimming pool in Absolut LA (Figure 4), a furnace in Absolut Pittsburgh and rain-covered tarmac in Absolut Seattle. For Chicago, known in the US as the Windy City, the elements on the face of the bottle are in the process of being blown away (Figure 5). To maintain this pace and keep the ideas fresh, everyone within the agency and the client inputs their ideas. Indeed such is the confidence of the agency and the client in the creative idea that more recent ads have dispensed with the bottle. Absolut Evidence just features a fingerprint, Absolut Subliminal has the brand name shadowed into some ice cubes and Absolut San Francisco has the bottle disappearing into the mist that the city is famous for. The tone of these ads is what has put Absolut ahead of the competition and kept them there. Peter Lubalin of TBWA says:

> We decided at the beginning that we can't be more authentic than Stolichnaya, but we can be more fashionable and sophisticated and contemporary, and more likeable.

LAUNCH OF CITRON AND PEPPAR

With the success of the main brand, Carillon decided to launch two brand variants: Citron — a citrus flavoured vodka and Peppar — a hot and spicy one. These products were bottled in the same distinctive shape and it therefore seemed logical to extend the Absolut campaign into these new tastes. However, although the advertising needed to borrow from the main brand heritage, there had to be sufficient differentiation, so that people would immediately recognise the product. This was achieved by using colour. The Peppar branding on the Absolut bottle is red and the overall background colour of all the Peppar advertising is red. The Absolut line in this instance is Absolut Peppar and the spiciness of the product is conveyed through such ads as the double page spread featuring the bottle on one side and its burnt out imprint on the other (Figure 6). In contrast, all Citron advertising uses a yellow green background to reflect the limes and lemons that are added to provide the taste. Such has been the impact of the new variants through the adaption of a well-tested formula that in 1989 Absolut Citron passed 100,000 case sales, making it the number three imported vodka in the US in its own right.

Results

The now seemingly humble objective of matching Stolichnaya's level of sales was achieved in 1986. By 1992, Absolut had 62 per cent of the 4.3 million case imported vodka category and it is now the number one selling imported spirit in any sector in the US. Although the overall vodka category has declined over the last decade, the imported sector has grown, mainly off the back of Absolut, but also through the proliferation of new imported brands, most from Northern Europe. In spite of the intensity of competition in the market, Absolut's growth shows no sign of waning.

Although there is always the danger that one day a new fashion brand may appear and eclipse Absolut, so far Carillon and TBWA have managed the difficult balancing act of being fashionable without appearing faddish. This is partly because Absolut's fashionability is under-pinned by a quality (and importantly perceived quality) product, which has been re-inforced by continually rotating the early quality ads with the more recent fashion versions. It is also partly because Absolut's advertising stands head and shoulders above its competitors in creating a desirable brand image. Not surprisingly the campaign has been richly rewarded by the advertising and media industry. Most notably, it has won the Kelly award for effective print advertising twice (1989 and 1991) — a distinction shared by only by one other advertiser: Nike. Its success has been enduring because, as Geoff Hayes says:

A lot of competitors are trying to duplicate the Absolut style of advertising, but they haven't worked out what the one thing in the Absolut advertising is that works: it's the quirkiness of the visual and the humour of the line. They think it's the big product shot. They didn't understand ten years ago and they still don't understand. They've missed the point.

Points to Note

- Market research said Absolut had nothing going for it. Carillon however, trusted to intuition and decided to ignore the research findings.

- A piece of simple but inspired creativity led to the development of a campaign, which focused on the importance of creating a fashionable image for the brand.

- The campaign has evolved and become more sophisticated over the years. This has ensured that the idea has continued to remain relevant and aspirational to consumers.

- The campaign has shown itself to be able to break new ground in the way that print media is used from naked bottles to snowflakes.

- Although there are product differences in Absolut's product formulation, the inability of consumers to distinguish one brand from another renders the differences irrelevant.

- Much of the campaign's success can be attributed to the close working relationship between Carillon and TBWA, in which both sides have contributed significantly to the creative process. Carillon have also been willing to outspend the competition and invest in the brand's long term development.

- The brand has broadened its consumer base to become the dominant force in the imported vodka sector of the market.

References

[1] Steve Blount & Lisa Walker with the American Association of Advertising Agencies. *The Best Advertising Campaigns*, Rockport, Massachusetts 1988

[2] Interview with Peter Lubalin, Creative Director, TBWA, July 1992

2

OSLO SPORVEIER

CHANGING ATTITUDES TO PUBLIC TRANSPORT

WHERE THE LIONS OF THE NIGHT MEET

In spite of the best efforts of national and local government to discourage the private motorist, the car remains the most popular form of transport in most European cities. For although we now recognise and experience congestion on the roads and environmental pollution, the convenience and privacy a car affords tend to overcome the irritations of driving and any notions of social responsibility.

In many cases, the alternative of public transport is found to be wanting. In London, dirty and overcrowded trains are hardly less stressful than driving at a rush hour average of 13 miles per hour on the roads. In Oslo, however, over the last decade, the consumption of public transport has increased. Partly this has been due to deliberate government policy. For example, motorists now have to pay an 11kr toll every time they enter the inner city ring and public transport has right of way over other road users. Perhaps more important, however, has been the focus on providing consumers with the service they want. Not an innovation in itself — London Underground used to have this kind of focus (now sadly lost) in the thirties — but an orientation that has been missing from many public services in the more recent past. The responsibility for the innovation of enhancing the provision of public transport in Oslo has been a uniquely close relationship between Oslo Sporveier (Public Transport) and their advertising agency of the last seven years, New Deal.

Background

In 1985, when New Deal first started working with Oslo Sporveier, the public transport system had an appalling reputation. It was old-fashioned, provided poor service and had no sense of customer focus. People used the service if they had to, rather than because it represented a good alternative to making a journey by car. Although this state of affairs was widely recognised, little had been done to correct it.

To get underneath this overall negative attitude, New Deal undertook a large piece of quantitative research which segmented the public into 17 different groups, who used public transport for a variety of reasons and consequently had distinct attitudes towards it. Some, such as commuters, used it every day and experienced on a regular basis the irritations of the service; social users travelled by public transport only occasionally and were less directly critical. However, what unified every audience was the perception of lack of quality in the public transport service. To correct this, the service had to be improved. The agency recognised that the image of a public transport company was primarily determined by the experience of using it. Advertising could help alter perceptions of Oslo Sporveier, but it would only have substance if the client improved the product in line with consumer needs. It was something that British Rail ignored when they developed their 1980s 'This is the age of the train' campaign — a claim which had little credibility with the travelling public.

The objectives of Oslo Sporveier were twofold. First, existing users had to be encouraged to increase their usage across the tram, bus and train network. Second, new users had to be encouraged to use the service. To tackle the first objective, the process of travelling had to be made easier. In 1985, there was only one place in Oslo where season tickets could be purchased. This inconvenience meant that people tended to travel on tickets bought on the tram or bus. Not only did this hamper the service by slowing it down, it also failed to motivate people to travel on public transport. Therefore, the company decided to sell season tickets through newsagents. The initiative was important, both because by making it easier to buy season tickets it would encourage people to use the transport network, and also because it would send a signal to the travelling public that the company was capable of change. From an advertising perspective, it gave the agency a product it could promote, rather than having to make a bland and unsubstantiated claim about the quality of service.

THE LAUNCH CAMPAIGN

Oslo Sporveier's historic means of communication was informative and worthy advertising in the press. This provided a rational reason for using public transport, but it did not create any empathy with the company. Almost inevitably, public transport is an irritant: buses get delayed, trams get overcrowded. It is important that these negatives are well managed, but it also means that advertising needs to concentrate on communicating in an emotional way the positive aspects of travelling. Indeed, just as British Rail's 'This is the age of the train' failed, so their 'Relax' campaign, which stressed the relative relaxation of rail travel, succeeded. Stressing the positives does not make the negatives go away, but it makes sure they are not at the front of the mind.

New Deal also recognised that print was going to be too restrictive if they were going to achieve that emotional link, and both change perceptions and promote the take-up of season tickets. There was no commercial television in Norway at the time, so the only viable alternative was to use cinema. Rather than trying to sell the idea conceptually to the client, New Deal decided to take a risk. They would write, direct and film the commercial themselves and then show the client the finished product. If the client rejected the ad, they would have to carry the cost. Not surprisingly there was tremendous pressure to produce something creatively distinctive that would connect with the consumer and to do it cheaply.

Knut Andresen, the Creative Director at New Deal, knew the budget limitation meant there could be no stylish lifestyle ads. The execution would have to be a short sketch which demonstrated the benefit of having a season ticket. The solution they came up with features a ticket collector on a bus asking for tickets. At the front of the bus is a smug looking, self-satisfied woman, who holds her ticket aloft ready for the collector. On the seat next to her is a punk, who just before the collector arrives snatches her ticket and eats it. As she looks aghast, he shows the collector his season ticket. The end frame says 'Smart people buy season tickets — not single tickets' (figure 1). Simple and effective and superbly cast, New Deal managed to make the film for £3,000 — mostly on

Figure 1 Oslo Sporveier's launch advertisement

the basis that the actors would only be paid if the client accepted the work. Knut Andresen describes the client's reaction to the film:

> The client was a bit confused, because he hadn't been given anything like it before. But when we showed it in cinemas, people were standing up and clapping; he said I don't understand. After that we had *carte blanche* to do what we wanted.

The ad was also popularly received by the advertising and media world. Buoyed up by the reaction of consumers, New Deal entered the film for the international advertising awards at Cannes. It won gold — probably making it the cheapest commercial ever to win a gold Lion there. In fact, it won awards all over the world and was featured on both Japanese and British TV, as well as being run free as a public service every day for two weeks on Norwegian TV.

NIGHT BUS

In spite of their success, Oslo Sporveier and New Deal knew they could not rest on their laurels. Having started the process of changing consumer perceptions, the pace had to be kept up. Also, the second objective of encouraging new users had to be addressed. The next product to be launched was the Night Bus. New Deal applied the same principles to this as to the punk ad. A well-cast and well-executed sketch would demonstrate in a humorous way that all types of people used buses. The ad features a man leaving the Theatre Café — a well-known and highly regarded restaurant in Oslo. On the way out he picks up his hat from the cloakroom; it is obviously someone else's, it is far too small and sits perched uneasily on top of his head. He gets on the night bus and sits next to a man with a far too large hat — the inference is obvious. The end frame reads, 'Where the lions of the night meet — Night Bus'. Although this only won a Bronze Lion at Cannes, the ad was extremely effective in encouraging people to use public transport services at night. It appealed to a different market segment from 'punk' but, like the first ad, Night Bus also served another role: to get people to re-appraise Oslo Sporveier as a means of transport and an alternative to car or taxi. Although the first two ads serve to make distinct messages, they are both obviously from the same campaign and have a continuity of tone based on the style of their humour.

DEVELOPING THE CAMPAIGN FURTHER

The development of the public transport campaign has continued to meet the objectives of communicating specific services or messages to both general and specific audiences, while building a consumer franchise through the improvement of the overall image of the company. Key to the improvement of the company's image has also been the impact of the advertising on the people who actually provide the service: the employees of Oslo Sporveier. If the people who drive the buses and trams do not believe in the strategy or cannot translate it into their own terms, then the ideal of a customer-oriented service will not succeed. After all, it is these people who deal with the general public on a day-to-day basis, and it is through them that service perceptions will be created — a fact that has long been recognised by airlines, who have stressed in advertising the role of the air stewardess.

Not surprisingly, New Deal's advertising has been enduringly popular. Even when the strategy has perhaps gone slightly off track, it has created a sense of unity between customer and employee against the car driver. For example, after the first two films the agency decided to encourage the use of public transport by re-inforcing people's irritation about traffic jams. This has been a well-tried route, not only in Norway. The ad New Deal produced, which was much glossier than the early work, shows cars jammed together in a slightly surrealistic setting with a background track of *Don't fence me in.* The execution does not have the same strong characterisation, nor does it do anything to help change attitudes towards Oslo Sporveier, but it does remind public transport users of the perils of car travel.

The next TV film which New Deal produced extended the union between users and staff. It set out to communicate a specific message: 'Remember to park at least 70cm away from the tram tracks,' and it used the reputation of Public Transport drivers as aggressors to advantage. Anecdotal evidence suggests, for example, that people in Oslo believe tram drivers don't take much care about whether they hit parked cars or not. However, because there is a sense of retributive justice in the ad, and because it is done with wit and charm, the viewer identifies with the tram driver rather than the Rockabilly motorist — one can imagine employees loving this ad (Figure 2). Knut Andresen also praises the client's courage in taking on the ad:

I think they (Oslo Sporveier) are the bravest client in Norway. The man in the hat — I can't imagine any other client going for it. They would all say people will think we're too aggressive, but the humour helps overcome this.

Again the ad is a sketch and it has the same quirky characterisation that has come to typify the Oslo Sporveier campaign. However, the ads are high-risk, because although they are very noticeable and create strong emotional links with the viewer, they have the undoubted potential to offend people and bring to the forefront people's prejudices.

More recent work has appeared on the new commercial TV channels in Norway. It has continued to address the general issues, such as the benefits in terms of time and money in using public transport, as well as specific triggers, such as appealing to people's concern with the environment. Although this would probably have little impact in Britain or in Southern Europe, it works effectively with the environmentally conscious Norwegians. The latest ad, for example, which does not travel particularly well, is a parody of religious meetings. It features an English speaking presenter who is hectoring his audience about the environmental consequences of car travel. His Norwegian translator, however, decides to tone down the message in the translation, thereby losing the sense of it. The humour comes from the response of the audience, who applaud the translator's version of the impassioned message.

As well as the popular television and cinema campaigns, the press has been used as a support medium in which the detail of the company's innovations has been put across. In contrast with the television work, the press campaign is much more serious and straightforward. For example, in line with the above television campaign on environmental pollution, there has been print advertising which has detailed the obvious advantage of electric trams over cars in this respect. However, it does not integrate tonally with the TV films and perhaps it misses an opportunity to re-inforce the messages communicated on screen.

Figure 2 Sporveier's hat trick

Results

Norway, like much of the industrialised world is now in recession and the consumption of public transport has been relatively static since 1990. However, its market share has actually been increasing as the total level of travel within Oslo has declined. In any case, the significant impact of the weather on travel makes the correlation between advertising and consumption difficult to judge. Nonetheless, New Deal have helped to develop Oslo Sporveier as a brand with a distinctive personality, which is undoubtedly popular with both employees and the public.

The company now features prominently in its planning an emphasis on customers and listening to their needs. It recognises that to become an attractive alternative to the car, legislation alone will not suffice. People have to want to use public transport in preference to their car. The only way to achieve this is continued innovation, such as the introduction in 1993 of credit card type season tickets, and better bus and tram frequency in peak times. However, the innovation has to be communicated and supported by an overall positive attitude towards the services offered. Here, the union between agency and client in producing highly noticeable and effective work is vital. The reputation of the company has improved considerably across a variety of measures since 1985 and in spite of government dictated price rises, use of public transport has been maintained. In addition, the better attitude towards the company has translated into two other very practical benefits. When the company runs TV or cinema advertising, vandalism decreases. Second, there is less fare evasion and greater use of season tickets. All this has been achieved, in relative terms, on very small budgets; providing the company can continue to enhance the provision of public transport, the longer term should see growth in the level of use of trams, buses and trains.

Points to Note

- Perceptions of public transport provision are largely determined by the direct experience of using them. The co-operation between Oslo Public Transport and the agency in developing a consumer-focused product was therefore key to improving the company's reputation.

- Inevitably, negatives will exist in the mind of the travelling public, because services will not always be on time (especially in a country like Norway where the weather is so influential). Advertising can help overcome the negatives by developing a positive emotional relationship with the service provided.

- Employees are an important audience for this type of advertising, because their attitudes and behaviour are one of the most visible aspects of the company.

- New Deal's advertising is risky and has the potential to offend some people, but it does create a very strong sense of corporate personality for Oslo Public Transport. This is advertising that people enjoy watching.

- The creation of a favourable image, has helped to improve the company's performance and also to reduce such specifics as fare evasion and vandalism.

3

PERSIL WASHING-UP LIQUID

TAKING ON PROCTER AND GAMBLE

ROBBIE COLTRANE AND HIS GRANNY

> The best of all ways to beat P & G is, of course, to market a better product.[1]

Sound advice, but no one has bettered Procter and Gamble (P & G) in washing-up liquids in the last 30 years. P & G's Fairy Liquid has dominated its sector in a way that is rare for packaged goods brands. It has built and maintained a market share in the UK in excess of 50 per cent. It has a superior product performance widely recognised by consumers, and a consistent approach to advertising which has concentrated on the two essential attributes of a brand in this market: efficiency and care. However, in spite of freezing prices at 1987 levels, spending £11.6 million on advertising in the year to May 1991, increasing the margins to the trade by 2 per cent, introducing banded packs along with other consumer promotions, and reformulating the product, Fairy's profitability is declining. Lever Brothers, part of Unilever, have upset the stability of the washing-up liquid market by playing their trump card: Persil.

Since the 1950s, Persil has been battling with Procter and Gamble brands — most notably Ariel — for dominance in the fabrics detergent market. Persil's positioning in this sector is a reflection of Fairy's in washing-up liquids and has been built upon a combination of performance and care. Performance has been communicated by focusing on results rather than process; care has been conveyed by trying to give the brand a human face. Advertising has concentrated on communicating family values, as represented by the Persil mum, who is ever-present in the TV commercials. Whereas Ariel is a tool for cleaning clothes, Persil (like other very British brands, such as Oxo) is a friendly product that appeals both functionally and emotionally to consumers.

In the early 1980s, the strength of Persil as a brand led Lever to wonder whether its attributes could be stretched to include a washing-up liquid. In spite of having two brands in this market — Sqezy and Sunlight — Lever had been unable to dent Fairy's share. After some ten years of research and soul-searching, Persil washing-up liquid was launched in September 1990 and achieved faster distribution than any grocery trade product to date. Given its initial success, it may seem surprising that Lever took so long to launch the product, but as Ev Jenkins, Planning Director at J Walter Thompson, London, points out, the risks were not inconsiderable:

> When you put a name like Persil on something, failure is not an option, because you damage the franchise you've got by having a public failure. It would affect your standing with the trade and with the consumer and would undermine your employees' morale.

DEVELOPING A COMPETITIVE PRODUCT

> Nielsen once examined the fifty three most successful new brands launched over a two year period, finding that the most important of eleven reasons for success was clearly functional performance.[2]

In the washing-up liquid market, Fairy has consistently set the performance standards around efficiency and care. The concentrated product formulation has historically been better than anything else on the market and people have understood, as a result of the advertising, that although you pay a bit more for Fairy than other brands, it is better value in the long run because it goes further. To compete effectively, Lever had to manufacture a product that at least achieved parity and preferably surpassed

Fairy. After much testing, Lever managed to create a formulation that out-performed Fairy in terms of number of plates washed and was perfumed in a distinctive way which appealed to consumers.

If Lever could get the caring message across as well, they would have an optimally positioned washing-up liquid. The Persil name was the obvious means of achieving this, because the brand already had this positioning in fabrics. Therefore the added values associated with Persil could be transferred across and, hopefully, achieve immediate recognition and acceptance by the consumer. This, along with the pack design, would be vital in the battle with Fairy, because it was recognised by Lever that Procter and Gamble would almost certainly reformulate their product in order to cut out Persil's advantage. Indeed, such was the importance that Lever attached to developing a distinctive brand that they delayed the product launch a year so as to allow for a new bottle-shape to be manufactured. Originally, Persil washing-up liquid was packed in a cylinder — the norm for liquids in the UK. However, Lever conducted tests which compared the performance and appeal of the tube against a waisted bottle. Although the waisted bottle is marginally less space-efficient on shelf, the figures for both trial and repeat purchase for it were higher.

THE CHINK IN FAIRY'S ARMOUR

For some ten years, Procter and Gamble have been running a TV campaign featuring the British actress, Nanette Newman. The various executions have tried to demonstrate that although Fairy is premium-priced, it is able to wash more dishes than other brands. The caring connotation of the long-running line used by Fairy, 'Hands that do dishes are as soft as your face', is still fondly recalled and forms the backbone of the Fairy brand. The campaign has been remarkably consistent and still records very high levels of spontaneous and prompted recall and Nanette Newman is a well-recognised spokesperson.[3] However, there is no proven link between recall and consumer attitudes and behaviour and it may be the case that consumers buy Fairy despite the advertising. Lever and J Walter Thompson certainly believed, as a result of their own research, that Fairy advertising was a fundamental weakness of the brand. Anne MacCaig of Lever says that 'while the Nanette Newman campaign is well understood and mild-green Fairy is recognised, it still grates on people.' Ev Jenkins adds:

> As soon as you start laboriously talking about product detail and process, women feel very patronised and very angered, and that's what we found with the Fairy advertising.

Indeed, there has been a shift in much fast-moving consumer goods (fmcg) advertising over the last few years, which seems to have been ignored by Procter and Gamble. Traditionally, the tone of voice and the kind of advertising produced in fmcg markets were concerned with communicating product benefits: the sort of advertising that speaks in 'manufacturingese' at consumers. However, as women have grown increasingly independent financially, more advertising literate and more confident as consumers, they seem less and less prepared to tolerate what many see as a patronising style of advertising.

Now some advertisers and their agencies have begun to develop a different type of advertising, which uses humour and intelligence to get the message across; which treats women as thinking consumers; which may use different triggers to capture their attention, but is consistent in quality with advertising to men. This is not to argue for humour for its own sake nor to suggest that all women have the same attitudes, but to argue for realism and to recognise the relative importance of various activities — such as washing clothes or doing the dishes — in the daily lives of most women.

DEVELOPING AN ADVERTISING APPROACH

The perceived weakness of Fairy's advertising, combined with the strength of all other aspects of the brand, made it doubly important that the Persil advertising was effective. Based on their test market results, Lever decided to set themselves a target of an 18 per cent long-term share of the market. To accomplish this required high levels of trial. The strength of the Persil name would be integral to achieving this, but it was also vital that the advertising itself helped stimulate consumers to switch from their existing brand repertoire. In particular, Lever identified Persil detergent users as most likely to switch. (Initial results indicate the validity of this: there has been a 25 per cent greater tendency of

Persil detergent buyers to use Persil washing up liquid than the norm.) Indeed, the relationship with the main brand was to be a key element in the development of the advertising.

Persil washing-up liquid has the same basic product benefits of efficiency and care as the detergents brand. Without this empathy, the use of the Persil name on the washing-up liquid would have the potential to confuse consumers. Lever determined that the new product would not only build on the main brand strengths and draw on the long-established Persil heritage, but would also add value to it. To achieve this, the advertising would have to relate to Persil fabrics advertising with its focal point of the mother, but also distance itself to communicate other values. It would have to create an identity for the product in its own right and, in a very practical sense, ensure that consumers did not purchase the washing-up liquid thinking it was detergent washing liquid.

J Walter Thompson's initial response was to develop a campaign using the Persil mum and family. The idea was based on the thought that no one likes to do the washing-up and therefore 'there is no nicer way to get a sparkling pile of dishes than somebody else's hand in the sink.'[4] The creative approach used humour to get the message across, because the tone of Persil advertising is to reflect real behaviour and perspectives, as opposed to those of the manufacturer. Therefore the best way to get the dishes done is to blackmail someone else — an idea that has to be treated with wit, lest it become threatening. This concept was put into qualitative research and seemed to perform well. Consumers, when prompted, also argued that you wouldn't confuse the washing-up liquid and the detergents brand.

However, there was a feeling among all involved in the project that the approach was simply too close to the detergents advertising. It was communicating the same values as the fabrics campaign and therefore could in no sense add another dimension to Persil as a brand. Thus JWT and Lever determined that the campaign needed to take the Persil fabric values and place them in an orbit that was clearly different. This raised the conundrum of how to use the focus of the fabrics advertising — the mother — and yet create something distinctive. The solution was to create 'Granny' as the surrogate mother with actor/comedian Robbie Coltrane as her surrogate son, Billy.

The new idea followed many of the principles of the first. It used humour to convey a series of messages about Persil washing-up liquid and was based on the idea that no one likes doing the washing-up. However, it distanced itself by parodying the fabrics advertising. Although the idea is built around the relationship of Granny and her grandson, rather than Coltrane himself, (Steve Martin was one of the early ideas for the role), he now appears to have been an inspired piece of casting. One year into the campaign he was recalled as Persil's man by 36 per cent of consumers and among 15–24 year olds by 53 per cent. However, when he was selected for the role he was less well-known and perhaps more of a gamble. He had starred in a popular TV series, *Tutti Frutti*, and in the film *Mona Lisa*, but *Nuns on the Run*, *The Pope Must Die* and his televised one man show were all in the future. To ensure the idea and Coltrane worked, JWT undertook some discussion groups using their initial scripts and clips from *Tutti Frutti* and *Mona Lisa* as prompts. The results seemed promising and Coltrane was not only credible, but to many women sexually appealing. The Coltrane execution was then tested against the original idea, and Coltrane emerged much the stronger of the two. Not only did he add an emotional appeal to the brand, he did so without getting in the way of the communication.

THE LAUNCH

To compete effectively with Fairy, three simple messages needed to be put across, along with a reassurance about the mildness of the product:

- Now Persil washes more than just your clothes.
- Persil washes more than you think.
- Persil is efficient.

Rather than trying to put across these performance and care ideas in one execution, it was agreed that they should be treated separately, with the thought that 'Persil now washes more than your clothes' providing the basis for the launch. One of the first TV executions (and the poster support for it) clearly makes the link between the fabrics detergent and the washing-up liquid by using the mnemonic of Granny hanging her plates on the washing line to dry. Billy (Robbie Coltrane) then runs out across the fields to help her bring them in when it starts to rain (Figure 1). The humour of the scene, with the lumbering Coltrane rushing to help his granny, sets the advertising far apart from Fairy and helps to create an emotional relationship between the consumer and the brand. In this execution, as in the others that followed, it is Granny who is controlling the larger-than-life Coltrane. It is always Coltrane who is doing the washing-up. As Fiona Inkley at J Walter Thompson says:

> There is a slight irreverence about all the advertising which shows that Persil understand how housewives feel about washing-up. And Robbie's perfect for that because he always looks cheesed off about having to do it.

Not surprisingly, Procter reacted aggressively to the Persil threat. Although Lever had anticipated a fierce response, they were not prepared for the promotional and advertising onslaught in support of Fairy. This escalated after the second phase of advertising, which concentrated clearly on the performance of Persil. Although Persil had a superior performance to Fairy, Lever initially used a top parity claim. However, after the initial burst, Lever used their superiority claim, 'the very best you can buy'. To counter this move, Fairy reformulated their product and complained to the ITVA. Persil and J Walter Thompson had finished up the film with two alternative voice-overs in anticipation of this. Although Persil subsequently reformulated, the claim was modified to 'one squirt of Persil gets it all done.' Rather than talking about the quantity of plates cleaned in the same way as Fairy, Persil has shifted its performance claim to focus on difficult cleaning jobs, such as greasy frying pans, Yorkshire puddings or even motor cycles (Figure 2). Such was the intensity of the battle that Lever spent £6.6 million in the year to May 1991 (*Media Register*), compared with £11.6 million for Fairy.

THE RESULTS

In awareness terms, Persil's advertising has been extremely successful. In research conducted in April 1991 for *Marketing's Adwatch*, prompted recall of Persil washing-up liquid was 71 per cent, compared with 70 per cent for Fairy. As already shown, the

BRAND: PERSIL WASHING UP LIQUID
DESCRIPTION: R.COLTRANE-HANGING OUT DISHES
TIME: 12:00:00   TRANSMITTED: Sunday 14th October 1990
DURATION: 00:30 secs   REGION: C4   FILE REF: 126516   PAGE: 1

sound; music and location effects

to end

male; OH GRAN GRAN NO

GRANNY

*GRAN GRAN
I THINK IT'S GOING TO RAIN*

2nd male; NOW PERSIL WASHES MORE

THAN JUST YOUR CLOTHES

AND MORE THAN ANY OTHER

WASHING UP LIQUID

......

IT'S THE VERY BEST YOU CAN BUY.

Figure 1 Helping granny out

BRAND: PERSIL WASHING UP LIQUID
DESCRIPTION: PT1: R.COLETRANE/MOTORBIKE
TIME: 20:22:00   TRANSMITTED: Sunday 4th August 1991
DURATION: 00:30 secs   REGION: THAMES   FILE REF: 135827   PAGE: 1

Figure 2 Difficult cleaning jobs

link between Coltrane and the brand is also strong. However, there are some caveats. Coltrane works best against men: 41 per cent of men link Coltrane with Persil compared with 32 per cent women. Although it is recognised that men are becoming more important in the decision-making process for washing-up liquids, it is still predominantly a female purchase. Also, there is a definite younger bias to the awareness of Coltrane, but this was anticipated and is no bad thing. Jeremy Stubbs, Advertising Manager of Lever, says:

> In research we were getting recall from far younger women, whose purchasing patterns are less well established.[5]

What is less easy to establish is whether the washing-up liquid campaign has added value to the main brand. With such a well-established brand as Persil, attitudes tend to be firmly entrenched and movements in dimensions such as 'contemporary and modern' are slow. However, in qualitative work JWT have picked up added excitement about Persil, as a result of Coltrane.

Sales have not yet achieved their target. The ongoing share by volume towards the end of the first year was approximately 12 per cent. However, in the five top retailers Persil briefly achieved a 31 per cent share. One of the problems has been in smaller retailers where Fairy's strong distribution has prevented Persil gaining sufficient shelf space. Moreover, it is recognised that Procter are better than Lever in this area, because of their willingness to provide tailor-made deals. Fairy's banded pack offer was also a clever tactical move, because apart from helping to stimulate sales, it helped to ensure the retention of existing shelf space. Shelf space is not the be-all and end-all, but achieving the 18 per cent share of the market will be difficult to achieve without it. The good news for Persil is that by May 1991 a 38 per cent repeat purchase figure had been achieved, which suggests that the brand has the capability to move from trial purchase into a regular item for a large number of consumers.

What has to be questioned is whether Procter and Gamble or Lever are making any money at the moment. P & G vowed to get Persil off the shelves within a year; they have failed. Although Persil has achieved very creditable results, it has not achieved its objectives. As Anne MacCaig of Lever says:

While we haven't reached our target figures yet [summer 1991] that seems mostly due to the fact that Cincinnati [Procter's Headquarters] has issued a blank cheque to support Fairy.

Ev Jenkins at JWT concurs: 'What we've succeeded in doing is creating the ultimate spoiling operation, where nobody makes any money.'

Both sides have too much to lose to back away from the confrontation. Lever have put one of their strongest brand names on the product; P & G in the UK rely extensively on Fairy for profit generation. Their latest move has been to introduce a reformulated product called Fairy Excel. The equilibrium of the market has been upset by the launch of Persil and the relaunch of Fairy, to the benefit of both retailers and consumers, but with little gain — so far — to either of the main protagonists.

Points To Note

- Using an established brand name for a new product confers existing values, but it is not without risks, especially if the new product fails.

- Competitor reaction to any new product launch needs to be carefully analysed, prior to making any commitment.

- Product performance is the key attribute of any successful brand.

- Humour and wit can be used to great effect in fmcg markets.

- Advertising is a vital component in the establishment of a brand personality and in encouraging trial.

- To achieve its sales targets, Persil will have to continue to improve the product and also start to develop an advertising tone and language that is distinctively different from Fairy's. It will have to break the rules that Fairy has established.

References

[1] David Ogilvy *Ogilvy on Advertising*, Crown Books, New York, 1983, p157
[2] John Philip Jones *What's in a Name?*, Lexington Books, 1986, p52
[3] *Marketing Adwatch*, 26 July 1991, records Nanette Newman as the second best recalled advertising spokesperson with 55 per cent
[4] JWT creative brief
[5] 'Coltrane has the first laugh on Fairy for Recall', *Marketing*, 26 July 1991

4

ROLLING STONE MAGAZINE

CHANGING MEDIA ATTITUDES

PERCEPTION AND REALITY

> It's hard for me to imagine life in America without *Rolling Stone*.[1]

Although *Rolling Stone* magazine has long been the dominant popular music magazine in America, it has made an equally important contribution as a questioning, iconoclastic, anti-Establishment voice in the often bland world of US journalism. Over the last 25 years, many of America's top writers and journalists — Tom Wolfe, Hunter S. Thompson, Joe Eszterhas, William Greider, P.J. O'Rourke — have contributed powerful and insightful views about contemporary society, politics, the arts and, of course, rock and roll. Jann Wenner, the publisher, says in the 25th Anniversary issue:

> When I started this publication — in a second floor loft above a small print shop in San Francisco — I wrote, '*Rolling Stone* is not just about the music, but also about the things the music embraces.' I began to interpret that charter rather broadly as time went on.[2]

The commitment both to music and to social and political criticism has been the magazine's strength. For example, amid the past media adoration of the Reagans and the Bushes, *Rolling Stone* stood out as a somewhat lonely voice in attacking their political cynicism. In taking this stance, the magazine sustained a perception that had been created in its early days: that its readership was revolutionary and anti-Establishment. The idea that *Rolling Stone* was a counter-culture, hippie publication may have had some credence in the late sixties and early seventies, when it was more overtly aimed at a politicised youth, but by the eighties the journalism, although still critical, had matured, as had the readership, which had become relatively affluent, predominantly male, 18 – 34 year olds.

MEDIA RESISTANCE TO *ROLLING STONE*

The problem with the perception that *Rolling Stone* readers were either impoverished hippies or ex-hippies was that advertising agencies and their clients were unwilling to put the magazine on their media schedules. They felt that the publication would add nothing to their spend and might positively harm their product's image. Even when *Rolling Stone* made it on to media planners' schedules, clients often asked for it to be removed.

To increase the amount of advertising revenue, *Rolling Stone* had to get advertisers and agencies to re-appraise their attitudes about the magazine. In 1985, the Minneapolis-based agency Fallon McElligott Rice (as it was then known) was invited by Jann Wenner to New York to discuss the problem.

CREATING PERCEPTION AND REALITY

Initially, *Rolling Stone* set Fallon McElligott the task of achieving a 10 per cent increase in 1985's total advertising pages over 1984's. To obtain this incremental business, a number of new target areas were defined: apparel, beverages, corporate accounts, personal grooming and automotive products. However, it became clear at the briefing meeting in New York that to increase the advertising revenue the problem of the misconception about the readership had to be addressed. While part of the Fallon team discussed the issue in *Rolling Stone*'s office, the creative duo, Bill Miller and Pat Burnham, retired to a coffee shop. As they talked about the meeting, Bill Miller started to scribble notes about the perceptions and reality of the *Rolling Stone* reader on a cocktail napkin:

> The idea for the perception and reality ads occurred to me that day in New York and was really born out of the thought that most people's thinking about *Rolling Stone* readers was

that they were into sex, drugs and rock and roll and all that that meant.[3]

If they could get the tone of creative work right, the Fallon team felt the *Rolling Stone* business was theirs. However, the agency had also just won the *Wall Street Journal* account. While the clients did not conflict in a competitive sense, they were such polar opposites (the conservative, Establishment *Wall Street Journal* versus the radical, anti-Establishment *Rolling Stone*) that there was a feeling among some people within the agency that one of the clients would have to be dropped. Bill Miller and Pat Burnham petitioned the agency management to keep *Rolling Stone* and sent Tom McElligott, the creative head, a direct mailer comprising a box with some rocks in it, with the line 'we'd like to get our rocks off on *Rolling Stone*.'

It was agreed that *Rolling Stone* and the *Wall Street Journal* could both stay. However, when Tom McElligott saw the ideas for perception and reality, he was dismissive. There was no headline in the ad and McElligott thought the meaning was too obscure. Bill Miller, though, had already done his small piece of market testing — he'd shown the ideas to the agency's media department, and they had understood it straight away. While Bill Miller worked up the ads with creative director Nancy Rice, other ideas were explored, but nothing seemed to work as well as the perception and reality concepts. With the meeting with *Rolling Stone* to present their work looming, the agency ran out of time to develop any alternatives. Although McElligott wasn't happy with the work, he agreed it should be shown to the client.

The first ads comprised a series of sixties icons who represented the perceptions of *Rolling Stone*, juxtaposed with their eighties counterparts, who represented the real *Rolling Stone* reader. Above the relevant image was placed simply 'perception', 'reality'. Underneath the right-hand 'reality' image was a concise piece of explanatory copy. The very first ad was a hippie looking reader compared with a yuppie-looking reader (Figure 1). The copy reads:

> If your idea of a *Rolling Stone* reader looks like a hold-out from the sixties, welcome to the eighties. *Rolling Stone* ranks number one in reaching concentrations of 18–34 readers with household incomes exceeding $25,000. When you buy *Rolling Stone*, you buy an audience that sets the trends and shapes the buying patterns for the most

Perception.

Figure 1 The first phase of the Rolling Stone
'Perception-Reality' campaign

Reality.

© Straight Arrow Publishers, Inc. 1987

If your idea of a Rolling Stone reader looks like a holdout from the 60's, welcome to the 80's. Rolling Stone ranks number one in reaching concentrations of 18-34 readers with household incomes exceeding $25,000. When you buy Rolling Stone, you buy an audience that sets the trends and shapes the buying patterns for the most affluent consumers in America. That's the kind of reality you can take to the bank.

Source: Simmons 1986

Rolling Stone

Perception.

Figure 2 Targeting women's products

Reality.

You no longer have to barbeque your underwear to assert your equality. For a new generation of female Rolling Stone readers, it's possible to be a feminist without giving up femininity. If your target market is women 18 to 34, your media plan will catch fire in the pages of Rolling Stone.

affluent consumers in America. That's the kind of reality you can take to the bank.

In addition to this type of generalised, 'ideological' ad, which Fallon McElligott hoped would help change the general perceptions of *Rolling Stone*, a number of category-specific ads were produced, targeted at those areas from which *Rolling Stone* thought it could gain advertising revenue. Among the initial executions was a VW van with a sports car, a keg of beer with imported beers and pocket change with credit cards.

When the work was first presented to Rolling Stone it created a mixed reaction.

> We presented a whole series of ads and they [*Rolling Stone*] were taken aback by it. I don't know what they expected, but this wasn't it. And it worried a couple of people in the room, but when it came to the key decision maker, the General Manager, Kent Brownridge, I remember him saying, 'I think it's fabulous'. I think he had a vision of what it could be before I did.[4]

Once *Rolling Stone*'s approval to the campaign was given, eight advertisements were worked up and placed in key advertising trade publications which would be read by both advertisers and agencies: *Advertising Age*, *AdWeek*, and *Marketing and Media Decisions*. The impact was almost immediate. In the first year of the campaign, advertising pages in *Rolling Stone* increased 25 per cent over the previous year. In the targeted product categories the results were even more dramatic — albeit starting from low bases. Awareness of and familiarity with *Rolling Stone*'s current reader profile was greatly improved among media decision makers and advertisers, and sales representatives reported back a much more positive selling environment. Jann Wenner was reported as saying that 'it was like someone came in with a wheelbarrow of money and dumped it on the floor.'

DEVELOPING THE CAMPAIGN

Having got the campaign off to such a successful start, the issue became how to sustain it. As the target market for the advertising and consequently the media choice was so clearly defined, the ads needed to be changed rapidly to sustain interest. Each ad would only appear two or three times before being replaced. Also, once the product category targets had been reached so quickly, there was a felt need to produce some more ideologically based advertisements and to target new areas, such as women's products. This resulted in advertisements such as the bras (figure 2) and, more recently, a map of Canada and an army recruitment leaflet. These ads are direct and quick to read and demonstrate the versatility of the core idea.

However, as the campaign has developed a number of problems have had to be faced up to. First, in many ways 'perception/reality' has become a victim of its own success. As attitudes have changed as a result of the advertising, so reality has become the perception. Media buyers and their clients see *Rolling Stone* readers not as hippies, but rather as young professionals. However, the ads have come to be viewed in a different way. Rather than trying to change attitudes, they serve to remind and have become icons in their own right. For example, readership of the ads has remained exceptionally high throughout the campaign, consistently scoring the highest recognition ratings of all advertising in particular issues of key trade magazines.

The viewing of the ads as pieces of advertising has also led to the idea that the advertising can become more oblique. As Art Director Mark Johnson says, 'Over time the attitudinal shifts have become more subtle and this needs to be reflected in the advertising.' However, although Fallon McElligott has tried to develop more cryptic executions, in general *Rolling Stone* has preferred to keep the communication direct. The advertising idea can sometimes raise a wry smile, but it only rarely challenges the reader's ingenuity.

The second problem is the shortage of relevant sixties icons. If the sole aim of the campaign was to juxtapose a sixties perception with an eighties reality, there would be no constraint. However, the advertising needs to be true to the ideas and principles of *Rolling Stone* and some of the crusades the magazine fought twenty years ago are still being fought today. For example, one of the creative team's ideas was a peace symbol (perception) with a Mercedes badge (reality). After the ad was presented, Jann Wenner wrote to Fallon about the idea. Bill Miller recalls:

> Jann wrote us a nice letter about that. He said we're still for peace at this magazine. I don't want everyone to think we're

selling that down the river.

Nonetheless, the campaign has now been going for seven years and the visual and verbal inventiveness has been sustained. There seems no reason why it shouldn't continue.

THE RESULTS

Rolling Stone is an example of a small budget campaign (approximately $500,000 a year, including all production costs) that has radically altered the way a specific target audience thinks about a product with which they were already familiar. As their perceptions changed, so did their behaviour. Since the beginning of the campaign through to the end of 1991, advertising pages in *Rolling Stone* have increased 58 per cent and the publication now competes very effectively for space on media schedules aimed at 18–34 year old men with such publications as *GQ*, *Sports Illustrated* and *Esquire*. Even more notable has been the ability to raise the average cost of advertising in *Rolling Stone*. Advertising revenues over the same period have increased 224 per cent. Particularly successful has been the number of advertising pages in the original targeted categories:

Apparel	+ 295%
Personal Grooming	+ 510%
Automotive	+ 83.5%

Qualitatively, the campaign has also been successful. There has been significant editorial coverage of 'perception reality' in *GQ*, *Advertising Age*, *Adweek*, *New York Times*, *Miami Herald*, *USA Today*, *Forbes*, National Public Radio and most recently on the *Today* show. *Adweek* has named *Rolling Stone* one of the ten hottest magazines for three of the last four years. And the campaign has won a whole host of advertising awards: Clios every year since 1986, gold medals in the One Show and the New York Art Directors' Club, and best print campaign of the decade (1980s) by the Board of Directors of the One Club. As Harish Bhandari of Fallon says, 'Perception/ Reality is one of the most revered campaigns in print advertising history'.

Points to Note

- *Rolling Stone* demonstrates the impact of a simple direct idea on a given target market.

- It demonstrates that successful advertising should work in two ways: immediately affecting attitudes and, in the longer term, helping to develop brand values.

- The impact of advertising, directly on sales, can be measured in campaigns that have a clearly identified target market where other external influences are minimal. Perception/Reality is a campaign that shows a change in attitudes leading to a change in behaviour.

- Advertising ideas that remain consistent over time often move from an initial requirement of creating awareness or changing attitudes to reminding and sustaining. They come to be seen as pieces of enjoyable advertising that reassure by their familiarity.

References

[1] Ed Bradley, Presenter, *60 Minutes*
[2] *Rolling Stone*, 11 June 1992, p31
[3] Bill Miller, Interview, 1 June 1992
[4] ibid.

5

SOLID FUEL

PROMOTING A DISADVANTAGED PRODUCT

FURRY FRIENDS

There are probably few products that enjoy such a competitive disadvantage as coal. As a source of domestic heating its rivals, primarily gas and electricity, enjoy a whole range of product advantages: cleaner, cheaper, easier to use, more efficient. It is perhaps not surprising then that, in spite of advertising support during the seventies and eighties, sales of coal as a main heating source headed consistently downwards. Logically, the solution to this should have been to maximise revenues from the declining domestic sector by increasing prices and reducing investment in marketing (the perfect cash cow), while building business in the commercial sector. However, in the late eighties British Coal, in the form of its marketing body — the Solid Fuel Advisory Service, ignored any such logic and asked a number of agencies to put forward their creative recommendations for an advertising campaign. One of the agencies was Saatchi & Saatchi.

INTERPRETING THE BRIEF

Solid Fuel provided all the competing agencies with a large amount of data about the domestic heating market. This quite clearly showed that there was a consistent decline in the use of coal as a main source of home heating. As people moved houses in increasing numbers during the boom years of the mid to late eighties, so they questioned their choice of heating. Invariably, because coal as a product was so disadvantaged, they found in favour of either gas or electricity. However, there was another sector of the market where coal did seem to possess some positive attributes. Supplementary heating, where people used coal fires in addition to central heating, was enjoying some growth among upmarket home-owners. This group were becoming increasingly home-oriented and appreciative of tradition. Whereas their parents had often sealed up fireplaces and replaced coal with easy-to-use electric fires, these people were opening up fireplaces and reverting to coal fires or lookalike gas fakes.

Saatchi looked at the two sectors and saw that it might be possible to slow down the rate of decline in the main heating sector. However, the lack of an overall positive attitude among consumers towards coal as a source of main heating meant that it would be difficult to use advertising to overcome all the negatives. In contrast, there was an existing interest in supplementary heating. Provided the right triggers could be found, this sector seemed to possess far more potential and Saatchi concluded that advertising should be concentrated here to capitalise on a developing consumer trend and fend off the competition from gas lookalike fires. However, the triggers were to prove hard to find.

UNDERSTANDING CONSUMER MOTIVATIONS

Saatchi conducted some twelve consumer group discussions for the purpose of the pitch. What the groups confirmed were all the negatives of the product: people thought of the nuisance of making up the fire, handling coal, cleaning away ashes, deliveries, storage and problems of non-delivery when there were strikes. Previous campaigns, such as coalmen merrily walking down the path, which had tried to overcome the negatives by creating empathy between the user and the product, in fact only served to remind people of the product's problems. However, the research also found that once consumers began to get into the idea of a real fire, they started talking emotionally about the benefits. They talked about real fires providing a different sort of heat, about creating a unique atmosphere, about something lacking in a room if the fire wasn't lit, and about a real fire turning a house into a home. Maggie Taylor, who was the Planning Director at the time, says:

> We identified it was no good trying to communicate any practical benefits of solid fuel — no matter how you tried to present it. It just kept triggering all the negatives. Through

research we determined we had to go an emotional route, because the end benefit was emotional and that was what people related to.

The task was therefore to find an approach that made an emotional appeal about the positives of a real fire without allowing consumers to think of the attendant negatives associated with coal.

THE IDEA FOR FURRY FRIENDS

The simple proposition that a real fire turns your house into a home was not easy to execute. Ideas were explored that developed out of the belief that people ritualised the firelighting process. However, in research this proved too close to problems of getting the fire to light. Alternatives were developed dramatising what it was like *not* to have a fire. This proved too obvious and rather negative with people who did not yet have fires. Also, the absence of fire meant that the executions were not making the most of the sensual and emotional qualities of a real fire. Simply showing an emotive image of a fireside also came over as rather bland and was rejected by consumers for being too obvious.

Adrian Kemsley, who was the Art Director on the pitch, then came up with the idea that fires could bring unlikely people together. One of the ads that came out of this thought was a script where Margaret Thatcher and Labour leader Neil Kinnock meet accidentally at an hotel with a roaring fire. Seduced by the atmosphere created by it, they end up dancing together. Whatever the rather practical difficulties of making such a film, the idea was not taken further, as a better idea soon emerged. Watching *Tom and Jerry* on TV one day, Kemsley came up with the idea of a dog, cat and mouse being seduced by a real fire. Not only were they more natural enemies than Thatcher and Kinnock, they were more likely to appeal on an emotional level to people considering an open fire.

The first script had the idea of a dog walking into a room and going up to sit by a roaring fire; then a cat would follow and sit next to the dog; and finally, the mouse would come and sit next to the cat. The voice-over would meanwhile extol the virtues of having a real fire in the home. Whereas the other ideas had stumbled at the research stage, Furry Friends was well received in consumer groups. Not only did it have simplicity and charm, but it also concentrated on the sensual qualities of a lit fire, thus largely avoiding the negative associations of coal. However, if Thatcher and Kinnock looked difficult to execute, Furry Friends was even more so.

MAKING FURRY FRIENDS

Saatchi & Saatchi felt they had come up with the idea to win the business; and so it was to prove. The animatic which had researched so well in consumer groups was presented as the main creative idea to the Solid Fuel Advisory Service. Paul Cowan, who was in charge of the pitch, remembers:

> They (Solid Fuel) had no reservations. They had all bought the strategy of needing to show the benefits of a real fire — even more than we did. So creatively, Furry Friends was an easy jump for them to make.

However, when it came to choosing a director to make the film, there were plenty of reservations. David Bailey was approached, but he felt he couldn't make the idea work; another director thought it could only be achieved by using special effects, while another felt the solution was to use people dressed up as animals. It was only when Adrian Kemsley met the then unknown commercials director, Tony Kaye, that he found someone who wanted to make the film as he did: as a naturalistic piece using real animals. Although Kaye was also making the award-winning British Rail ads for Saatchi at the time, there was some scepticism about his ability to deliver the quality the Saatchi team were looking for. However, in the absence of any alternatives, they took a gamble on him.

Although Kemsley had an agreed script and animation, certain aspects of the idea were to change during filming. Initially, the idea was to use a St Bernard as the dog, but Tony Kaye thought it would be more incongruous, and therefore more impactful, if the dog looked really vicious — as he does in *Tom and Jerry*. A casting session was held of vicious-looking dogs and a British Bulldog called Matthew was chosen, not so much because he looked vicious, but because he was ugly and his face had plenty of character.

To get the dog and the cat used to each other, they lived in the same home during the pre-production phase. When it came to filming, the dog and cat were perfectly natural with each other, but a way had to be found of communicating the romance, sparked off by the real fire, between such natural enemies. This idea had been addressed in the animatic by using heart shapes in the air around the animals. However, if the naturalism of the film were to be preserved, the animals actually needed to kiss each other. With the cat and the dog, this proved to be relatively simple. Fish paste was put behind the dog's ear, so that when the cat walked in and sat beside the dog, it licked the dog's ear. Mice, however, cannot be trained in the same way. To get round this, the mouse was put under a paper cup and placed next to the cat. The cup was then lifted, leaving a blinking and confused mouse next to the cat. The stroke of luck was that the cat then did a nose-to-nose double-take, giving the impression (once the sound effects were added) that the cat was kissing the mouse. The mouse then backed away from the cat. Once the film was reversed, it looked as if the mouse had walked up and sat down next to the cat. Contrary to popular myth, the mouse was not eaten by the cat, although it did have to be saved from the bulldog.

During production, it was also felt that the voice-over talking about the benefits of a fire was hindering rather than helping the communication. Rather than let the consumer concentrate on imagining the sensual pleasures of a fire, it was breaking the spell and serving to remind the consumer about the negatives. It was decided that the voice-over should be discarded and replaced with a soundtrack. Two ideas were shortlisted: Frank Sinatra singing *Strangers in the night* and the Shirelles singing *Will you still love me tomorrow?* Adrian Kemsley explains how the final choice was made:

> We knew we had a great film, but in this case the soundtrack was just as important as the visual. The big debate was whether the music was taking away from or enhancing the visual. It was thought that *Strangers in the night* was too big, too well known and Charlie Saatchi wanted the *Will you still love me tomorrow?* And Charles Saatchi obviously gets what he wants.

To compensate for the absence of a voice-over, the final frame simply said 'Now you know what people see in a Real Fire.' The use of 'Real Fire' served to provide both a point of distinction from gas lookalike fires and also avoided mention of 'coal' with all its taboo connotations.

THE NEW CAMPAIGN

The final film (Figure 1) has undoubted charm and in a succinct way communicates the emotional values about fires that consumers had talked about in the research groups. Although the first year's budget was only £2 million (versus approximately £15 million for gas and £15 million for electricity), the campaign achieved considerable additional coverage. It was written about in the national press and was featured on TV in such programmes as *Wogan* and *Jasper Carrot*. The Shirelles' *Will you still love me tomorrow?* was re-released by their record company and Athena printed and sold supporting posters in their shops. The results were impressive:

- Awareness of Solid Fuel advertising increased dramatically, to an index of 6. This is double the average awareness index of 3 for all advertising and well ahead of the higher spending gas and electricity campaigns, whose indices were at 1 and 2 respectively.

- Solid Fuel fires became more 'top of mind' as a form of heating people would consider. There was an increase of 12 per cent in the number of people saying they would like to have a real fire.

- The negative associations of Solid Fuel, such as 'dirty', 'hard work', declined.

- The positive associations, such as 'warmth', 'cosiness', 'relaxation', 'enhances the look of your home', 'brings people together', had doubled the number of people agreeing with the statements following the advertising campaign.

- High numbers of people said that they (a) enjoyed the advertising, (b) wanted to see it again and (c) believed it was out of the ordinary.

(Source: Millward Brown Market Research)

- *Today* newspaper readers voted it their favourite advertisement of 1988.

Figure 1 Solid fuel launch campaign

- The campaign won Golds at the Cannes Advertising Film Festival, British TV Awards, Creative Circle and the One Show and a Silver D & AD.

Although it is impossible to judge the real impact on sales because weather is the key influencer, coal merchants reported back an increased number of enquiries as a result of the campaign (and also requests from customers for posters of the Furry Friends). Indeed, such has been the enduring popularity of the campaign that it still gets talked about in consumer groups as an all-time favourite advertisement.

DEVELOPING THE CAMPAIGN

Having achieved a huge success with 'Furry Friends', the question arose as to how the campaign should be developed. The obvious route would have to been to do a variant on the dog, cat and mouse, but the Saatchi team felt that any extension of the original idea would simply pale by comparison; that the fluke of showing the animals kissing could not be bettered; and that a similar idea would require stunts which would lose the natural appeal of the interaction between the animals. Rather than feature the same characters, it was felt that the strategy of natural enemies seduced by a real fire needed to find a new milieu. Not only would this show the flexibility of the original campaign idea, it would also provide the opportunity to do something new and distinctive.

A whole new batch of executions was developed, featuring grizzly bears, a fox and hounds, a farmyard scene with a chicken and a child in a lodge in the Masai Mara with snakes and spiders. None of these seemed to work in quite the same way as 'Furry Friends', but the Masai Mara idea was taken a step further when Adrian Kemsley came across a photograph of a young boy playing with his pet snake in the wilds of Borneo. A new script was developed with the boy in a bath in front of a roaring fire; a snake enters menacingly and then joins the boy in his bath. 'Now you know what people see in a Real Fire' was again the end frame.

Whereas 'Furry Friends' was seen by people within Saatchi as inspired, there was great scepticism about 'Snake'. Part of the appeal of the dog, cat and mouse was their likeability as animals; in general, people don't feel the same warmth towards snakes!

Adrian Kemsley felt that this was part of the challenge and with Tony Kaye, he worked on shooting a beautiful film where the lighting would communicate the same sensuality achieved with 'Furry Friends'. The finished ad was indeed praised for the quality of the filming and when it was launched it created enormous impact and, like 'Furry Friends', obtained considerable press coverage. However there were a substantial number of people who hated snakes and the ITCA received a deluge of mail from angry TV watchers who were upset by the ad. Inevitably, the ITCA asked for the ad to be withdrawn and it was replaced by the original 'Furry Friends'.

THE RIGHT STRATEGY?

Although 'Furry Friends' continued for a while and there was a subsequent update of the execution, the structure of the Solid Fuel Advisory Service began to be questioned by British Coal. British Coal, who funded Solid Fuel, began increasingly to see themselves as a manufacturer, not a marketer. They felt marketing should be left to the distributors in the marketplace, rather than the producer. Achieving deals with the power generators, National Power and PowerGen, would determine the survival of British Coal, not their performance in the domestic market. Consequently the Solid Fuel Advisory Service, starved of funding, ceased to exist in the same way. However, those deals have been difficult for British Coal to achieve and the coal industry now employs only 41,000 miners in 50 pits, compared with 220,000 in 169 pits in the mid-1980s. If planned reductions go ahead, the industry will be a fraction of its former size by the mid-1990s. Although the industry is now more efficient than it once was, the manufacturing strategy has led to a dangerous reliance on the two power generators. A marketing led strategy, which looked for opportunities in commercial and domestic markets, might well have been more successful. Certainly the experience of British Steel, shows it can be done — in spite of political interference.

Although the domestic market was and remains, in relative terms, small, the original marketing strategy of focusing on supplementary heating, where there was a defined opportunity, still looks to have been well founded. And undoubtedly, 'Furry Friends' was an inspired piece of advertising creativity which met all the objectives set for it. In contrast, although 'Snake' was beautifully shot, it does not have the simplicity and charm of the original and is too far removed from the everyday experiences of the target market. It fails to connect. That the campaign was never developed to its full potential was due to a combination of changes in people[1], structures and strategies and ultimately perhaps to the difficulty of sustaining the creative excellence achieved with 'Furry Friends.'

Points to Note

- Coal is an example of a disadvantaged product, where the only hope of using advertising to good effect is by using emotional arguments to overcome rational negatives.
- Having determined the strategy, everything was sacrificed to creating advertising with a strong emotional appeal to consumers.
- The use of 'real fire' helped to create a brand identity.
- The dog, cat and mouse connected on an emotional level. Although the snake had impact, it did not connect in the same way.

References

[1] In 1990, Paul Cowan, Adrian Kemsley and Maggie Taylor left Saatchi & Saatchi to form their own agency, Cowan Kemsley Taylor

6

AIDS AWARENESS IN THE UK

CHANGING A NATION'S ATTITUDES

ICEBERGS AND TOMBSTONES

There are as many views on AIDS advertising as there are theories and ideas about the disease itself. Not surprisingly, adherence to a particular theory often determines reactions to the advertising. For example, if we believe, as much of the evidence in the UK suggests, that AIDS is a disease that attacks identifiable groups such as homosexuals and intravenous drug users, then the British government's mid-1980s campaign, which was initially targeted at the whole population, appears to have lacked focus. Alternatively, we can take the view, which is sustained by research done in some American cities and in the Bahamas, that AIDS can and does affect whole societies where cultural norms and social attitudes encourage the mix of drug abuse and sexual promiscuity. Then perhaps we have to take the view that the UK campaign was right to define the target market so broadly. What is certain is that we can reflect on the effectiveness in the light of the build-up of data over the last six years. In 1986, when the Government launched its campaign to achieve universal awareness of the disease, there was considerably less information and decisions had to be taken in the light of the best guesses of the medical establishment.

THE POLITICAL ENVIRONMENT

In 1986, AIDS was beginning to be a serious social and political issue. Over 500 cases of AIDS had been diagnosed and estimates on HIV (human immuno-deficiency virus), which is the cause of

AIDS, were estimated at between 30,000 and 40,000. The government also possessed a breakdown of AIDS cases, which suggested that in England and Wales over 90 per cent were either homosexual or bisexual, while in Scotland 60 per cent were drug misusers. In spite of the high levels of prevalence among these well-defined segments, there were two factors that worried the government about the spread of AIDS. First, in Africa, transmission was mainly through heterosexual intercourse, and there were almost as many women infected as men. Second, the long lead time, then estimated at about five years on average between becoming HIV positive and becoming ill, made assessment of the development of AIDS difficult. Then, as now, there were many unknowns. And of course there was no cure. Norman Fowler, who in 1986 had become Secretary of State at the Department of Health and Social Security, led his January 1987 statement at the AIDS conference with:

> There is no doubt at all about the importance of the public education campaign. The reality is that at present we have no medical defences against AIDS. There is no vaccine and no cure. And the experts agree that an effective vaccine is not expected within five years — if then. That is why public education is the only vaccine we have.

Norman Fowler had been convinced of the seriousness of the situation by the Chief Medical Officer, Sir Donald Acheson. Acheson had been looking at the problem in other countries and talking about the spread of the AIDS virus with the World Health Organisation. To halt the virus in Britain, he had come to the view that the only way forward was a public education campaign. People's attitudes and behaviour had to be changed.

THE FIRST PUBLIC EDUCATION CAMPAIGN

The first attempts at advertising were not very effective. They consisted of a series of press advertisements that were fairly inaccessible and also medical in tone (Figure 1). However, they were the first halting attempts by the government to tackle the issue and they did have the side-effect of prompting Sammy Harari, who had recently joined the advertising agency TBWA, to contact Norman Fowler. Harari, who had worked on the Government's anti-drugs campaign, knew that the Department of

AIDS. HOW TO KEEP YOURSELF SAFE.

AIDS is a serious disease. Not all the information available has been entirely accurate, so many people are confused about who is at risk, how the disease is spread and how dangerous it is.
To explain the facts entirely, it is necessary to describe certain sexual practices. These may shock but should not offend you as we are talking about an urgent medical problem.
Please read this carefully. It is up-to-date and authoritative. It is only by knowing the true facts about AIDS that we can hope to control the spread of this disease. This requires an effort by all of us.

DR. DONALD ACHESON   DR G CROMPTON

DR. IAIN S. MACDONALD   DR R.J. WEIR

CHIEF MEDICAL OFFICERS TO THE HEALTH DEPARTMENTS OF THE UNITED KINGDOM

WHAT IS AIDS?

AIDS stands for Acquired Immune Deficiency Syndrome.

It is caused by a virus that attacks the body's natural defence system.

This is why some people who have the virus can fall prey to infections and other illnesses which rarely trouble healthy people.

Not everyone who carries the virus develops AIDS. But, anyone who has the virus can pass it on.

At present there is neither a vaccine to prevent people catching the virus nor a cure for those who develop AIDS.

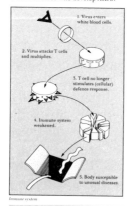

1. Virus enters white blood cells.

2. Virus attacks T cells and multiplies.

5. T cell no longer stimulates (cellular) defence response.

4. Immune system weakened.

5. Body susceptible to unusual diseases.

Immune system

HOW IS AIDS SPREAD?

In two ways.
❑ The virus spreads mostly through sexual intercourse with an infected person.
❑ It is also spread if an infected person's blood gets into someone else's blood. The major risk of this happening is to drug users who share needles or other equipment.
❑ Babies of infected mothers are also at risk, in the womb, during birth, or from breast milk.

DOES AIDS ONLY AFFECT HOMOSEXUALS?

NO.

HOW DO YOU KNOW IF YOU ARE AT RISK?

Injecting drug users are at risk if they share needles or other equipment. By far the best solution is not to inject at all. Those who persist, should not share equipment.

However, the major risk of infection is through sex.

The more sexual partners someone has the more likely they are to have sex with an infected person.

Cutting down on casual relationships cuts down the risk.

The next line of defence is to know what is safe sexual practice and what is not.

WHAT IS SAFE SEX?

❑ Any sex between two people who are uninfected is completely safe.
❑ Hugging, squeezing and feeling are all safe with anyone.

WHAT IS RISKY SEX?

❑ Sexual intercourse with an infected person is risky.
❑ Using a sheath reduces the risk of AIDS and other diseases.
❑ Rectal sex involves the highest risk **and should be avoided.**
❑ Any act that damages the penis, vagina, anus or mouth is dangerous particularly if it causes bleeding.
❑ Intimate kissing with an infected person may be risky.

IS AIDS SPREAD THROUGH NORMAL CONTACT WITH OTHER PEOPLE?

AIDS is caused by a virus which is spread by having sex with an infected person or by injection of contaminated blood. So normal social contact with a person who carries the virus such as shaking hands, hugging and social kissing carries no risk. Nor does being at school or at work with infected people.

IS AIDS SPREAD BY OBJECTS TOUCHED BY INFECTED PEOPLE?

No-one has ever become infected from toilet seats, door knobs, clothes, towels, swimming pools, food, cups, cutlery or glasses.

ARE BLOOD TRANSFUSIONS SAFE?

Before the virus was discovered, there was a very small risk from blood transfusions. Now all blood donations are screened for the infection. Any blood found to be infected is rejected.

The process of giving blood is not and never has been risky. All the equipment at blood donation centres is sterile and used once only.

WHAT OF THE FUTURE?

Doctors and scientists around the world are searching urgently for a vaccine or cure.

No-one can predict when this might be found, but it is almost certain it will take some time yet.

But AIDS can be controlled by reducing the spread of infection.

These facts show how it can be done.

MORE INFORMATION

For the booklet on AIDS, containing more detailed information and advice, write to Dept A, P.O. Box 100, Milton Keynes MK1 1TX.

Or call in strict confidence.

THE HEALTHLINE TELEPHONE SERVICE:
01-981 2717, 01-980 7222
or 0345 581151.

If you are calling from outside London, use the 0345 number and you will be charged at local rates.

DON'T AID AIDS

ISSUED BY THE DEPARTMENT OF HEALTH AND SOCIAL SECURITY

Figure 1 The first halting attempts at AIDS awareness

Health's advertisements would not work quickly or effectively enough. He says:

> I think the ads from the first campaign were ineffectual, because they were invisible. They didn't point out the essential. They were very worthy ads, but as the research from the end of 1986 bears out, you needed to jolt people into being aware of the problem.

Following Harari's approach a small team comprising Norman Fowler, Sir Donald Acheson, Romola Christopherson (Director of Information at the Department of Health) and Harari himself was put together to drive a new campaign forward. They saw the advertising objective quite specifically as raising awareness of the disease.

Part of the process of determining the direction future communications would take involved looking at the advertising that had been done abroad. The work that was appearing in Scandinavia was quite explicit, while other countries, including the USA, adopted a softer approach. Literature had also been produced in a variety of countries including Austria, West Germany, Switzerland and Greece. Although, because of British prudence, the government was not prepared to be as overt as the Scandinavians, the view (which was borne out by research) was that communications needed to be fairly explicit, if the message was to be put across precisely and with urgency.

The first part of the process of raising awareness among the population at large was the production of a leaflet which could be distributed to all 23 million households in the UK. This had been under way since the middle of 1986, but as Romola Christopherson says, it wasn't in an ideal form:

> There was a draft of the leaflet when I arrived, which smacked of being a product of a concerned bureaucracy and the views of a multiplicity of experts. The copy in communication terms was bad.

TBWA reworked the copy and then it was pored over, word by word, by the campaign team. The aim was to be sufficiently explicit to get the message across without unduly frightening people. TBWA also added the campaign slogan 'Don't die of Ignorance', which was a result of consumer research showing that the majority of people didn't know about AIDS and weren't too concerned when they did. The line formed the basis of a major national press campaign in the autumn of 1986, which was much more urgent than any previous work. Also, to help support the leaflet drop which was due to take place in early January 1987 and generate higher levels of awareness quickly, the group decided to produce some TV advertising.

The difficulty was the lack of specific guidance on what one could and could not do when advertising something like AIDS on television. However, it was felt to be inappropriate to try and include too much detailed information. Not only was TV the wrong medium to do this, but the real aim was to make sure people didn't throw away the leaflet — it contained over a thousand words of detail. Rather than trying to personalise the TV message by using people, it was felt at this point that dramatic imagery was required to try and communicate the sense of urgency. The first TV idea to be developed and presented was the monolith (Figure 2). This showed the chiselling of a tombstone with the word 'AIDS' emblazoned across the top. The end frame featured flowers alongside the leaflet. The second accompanying ad was the iceberg (Figure 3), which suggested that the people who had died of AIDS were just the tip of the iceberg. When the first cuts of the films were shown to Norman Fowler, he objected to both content and style. He felt that they were:

- a bit too feature film in style; too 'Hollywood'
- too wordy
- too explicit for mass media in talking about condoms
- too phallic, ie the drill sequence in 'monolith'.

The films were taken away and recut. A revised version was then presented by Sammy Harari to the Whitelaw committee, which was co-ordinating the government's AIDS strategy. Now,

- the copy was simpler and more focused
- the end line of 'Don't die of ignorance' was introduced
- the drill sequence was altered to avoid any suggestion of innuendo
- the overall noise level was reduced
- the reference to condom was taken out (although it was later put back in the iceberg film).

TELEVISION

THERE IS NOW A DANGER THAT HAS BECOME A
THREAT TO US ALL.

IT IS A DEADLY DISEASE AND THERE IS NO
KNOWN CURE.

THE VIRUS CAN BE PASSED DURING . .

SEXUAL INTERCOURSE WITH AN INFECTED
PERSON. ANYONE CAN GET IT, MAN OR WOMAN.

SO FAR IT'S BEEN CONFINED TO SMALL GROUPS
BUT IT'S SPREADING.

SO PROTECT YOURSELF . . .

AND READ THIS LEAFLET WHEN IT ARRIVES.

IF YOU IGNORE AIDS IT COULD BE THE DEATH OF
YOU.

SO DON'T DIE OF IGNORANCE.

ISSUED BY THE HEALTH DEPARTMENTS OF THE
UNITED KINGDOM.

Figure 2 Communicating the sense of urgency

TELEVISION

THERE IS NOW A DEADLY VIRUS WHICH ANYONE CAN CATCH FROM SEX WITH AN INFECTED PERSON.

BUT YOU CAN'T ALWAYS TELL IF SOMEONE IS INFECTED.

AND UNLESS WE'RE ALL A LOT MORE CAREFUL, THE PEOPLE WHO'VE DIED SO FAR WILL BE JUST THE TIP OF THE ICEBERG.

SO PROTECT YOURSELF.
IT'S SAFER IF YOU USE A CONDOM.

AND REMEMBER
THE MORE SEXUAL PARTNERS,
THE GREATER THE RISK.

Figure 3 Dramatic imagery was used to increase the impact

The committee was very concerned about the political context of what they were doing, so it was by no means clear that approval would be given for the films, but after some discussion it was agreed that the campaign could proceed. The final resultant ads were not subtle — they were powerful, dramatic and urgent. And perhaps not surprisingly, they were much criticised for being too frightening and causing people alarm. Getting the balance right was always likely to be difficult, especially given the variety of political, medical and social constraints. However, the question has to be posed whether a more personalised campaign might have worked harder and empathised with people's lives. Also, given the rapid change in attitudes and awareness that was taking place, the need to simply heighten awareness was quickly becoming irrelevant. Sammy Harari's view is that 'iceberg' and 'monolith' was the best possible work in the circumstances and the prevailing uncertainty about explicitness.

Whatever our retrospective judgement about the campaign, at the time media interest in the advertising was intense. To capitalise on this, the TV executions were launched at a press conference. Norman Fowler started the press conference with the background to the work and then Sammy Harari went through the details and presented the films. Such was the success of the approach in gaining editorial and magnifying the effect of the advertising that the routine was repeated with each phase of the campaign.

THE INITIAL RESULTS

The volume of research undertaken in the course of the campaign was phenomenal. There were several reasons for this:

- The target markets were diverse and had very specific needs.
- The nature of the subject was sensitive and fraught with taboo and therefore needed to be probed by a variety of research methods.
- There would be no second chances if the ads were wrongly directed.
- The nuances of language and their impact on people were subtle.

- The campaign was so visible that there had to be an authoritative body of research that could be pointed to, if the work were challenged.

In qualitative work alone, 160 depth interviews and 150 group discussions were commissioned by the Central Office of Information (COI). Additionally, four waves of samples of 700 adults were interviewed by the British Market Research Bureau (BMRB) between February 1986 and February 1987, with additional studies of homosexuals and young people between 13 and 21. The following are selected from the results of that research:

- Over the year the proportion of people who claimed to have seen or heard or read anything about AIDS, doubled from 44 per cent to 94 per cent of the adult population.

- Proven recall of advertising was 87 per cent for gays and 82 per cent for the general public and 78 per cent for the youth sample: *'the highest figures we [BMRB] know of for any social persuasion advertising campaign in Britain'*.

- The universal household leaflet was seen by 82 per cent of adults, 82 per cent of the youth sample and 76 per cent of gays.

- The proportion of people claiming to know more about AIDS than a couple of months previously rose from 38 per cent to 70 per cent among adults over the four waves and from 60 per cent to 84 per cent among the youth sample between waves 3 and 4.

- *'It is concluded that the 1987 advertising campaign has substantially achieved the objective of being noticed and stimulating discussion.'*

AIDS AND DRUG ABUSE

The 'iceberg' and 'monolith', the accompanying leaflet and press and poster support helped to achieve the first objective of the campaign against AIDS, which was to make the public aware of the problem. This process was abetted by National AIDS Week, which was an idea generated by the working group who felt that the advertising should be the catalyst for wider discussion. For one week both the BBC and ITV produced a range of programmes about AIDS, which created a national debate about AIDS.

However, having started with a broadly based campaign, the government now began to focus its attentions on the sections of the population most at risk. The gay community was already very aware of the issue, partly because the Terrence Higgins Trust had been so active in the area. The problem of drug abuse among young people and the transmission of AIDS through the sharing of needles remained. The government decided therefore to develop advertising aimed at dissuading young people from sharing needles and informing them about the dangers of AIDS if they did.

Again, the debate about explicitness surfaced. Scare tactics in health advertising can have one of two effects. Either the impact is such that it forces people to confront uncomfortable truths or, as some of the evidence suggests, rather than getting people to change their habits, it can close their minds. Or worse, if the tone is wrong, it has the potential to stimulate people to experiment. However, the qualitative research that the COI commissioned showed that among both the non-users (who needed to be supported in their resolve) and the users (who needed to be encouraged to seek support) there was greater credibility for advertising that confronted the issue head-on.

With a much more defined target market, there was also less pressure to tone the message down. Part of the difficulty in producing the 'iceberg' and 'monolith' advertising was the breadth of the target market: everyone from a teenager to a grandmother living in Brighton. Not only was it impossible to use a common colloquialism, there was also a real danger of a moral and political backlash from moralists, such as happened when James Anderton, Chief Constable of Greater Manchester said:

> Why do these people [homosexuals] freely engage in sodomy and other obnoxious practices, knowing the dangers involved ? These are the questions we should ask instead of publicising the wearing of condoms.

The anti-drugs and AIDS work developed by TBWA was provocative and personalised and is possessed of a confidence that is perhaps lacking in earlier work. The press and poster campaign used street language, such as 'smack' and 'fix', showed bloody needles and scarred arms and also the dirt, grime and general seediness associated with drug culture. The images, by war photographer Don McCullin and Clive Arrowsmith, are full of the realism for which they are famous. The work came through group discussions relatively unscathed, but there was considerable doubt as to how ministers would react to a poster featuring a filthy and bloody needle with the line, 'It only takes one prick to give you AIDS' (Figure 4). However, perhaps now used to provocative work, the Whitelaw committee gave its approval to both the press and poster work and the TV executions, which also overtly made the connection between AIDS and drugs. Ideas such as a boy being told by his doctor that he was HIV positive and then in flashback remembering the occasion he shared needles, or a boy at a party urging his girlfriend to try heroin, are simple 'slice of life' scenes, which demonstrate how needle sharing can lead to AIDS. They do not have the urgency of the previous work, but they are strong pieces of communication nonetheless; something that was borne out by the evaluative research.

EVALUATING 'DON'T INJECT AIDS'

The 'Don't inject AIDS' campaign had a budget of less than £3 million for 1987 — a not insignificant sum of money, but relatively small when compared to the £30 million the Government spent on promoting the privatisation of British Gas. However, it was extremely successful against most parameters. Researchers, Andrew Irving Associates, found that the campaign appeared to have strengthened the negative beliefs about heroin and also reduced the desire to experiment among younger drug users. Specifically, they noted the 'following positive effects might be attributed to the campaign:

- Heroin's image is now deflated and it has almost no positive appeal;
- it has increased the barrier between heroin and other drugs;
- it has linked heroin trial with an AIDS risk.'

However, there was a potential negative. Some of the evidence suggested that by overtly associating AIDS with heroin, there was a danger that heterosexual, non-intravenous drug users would believe AIDS was nothing to do with them: 'Only gays and junkies get AIDS'. So although the campaign may have done its work in frightening non-users off drugs, it may have dampened the connection between sexual promiscuity and AIDS. To address this

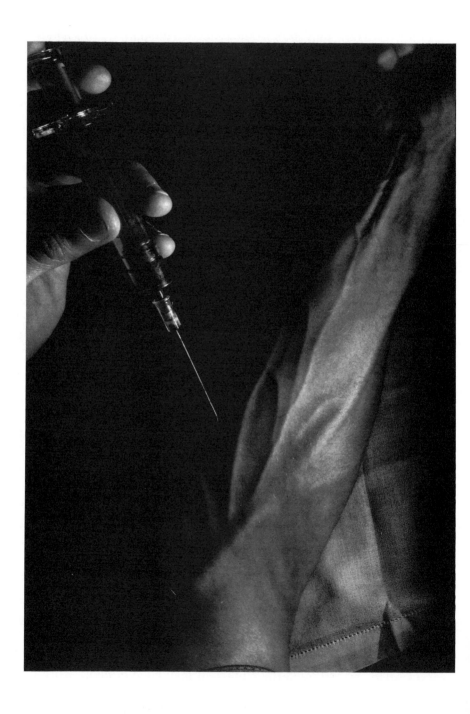

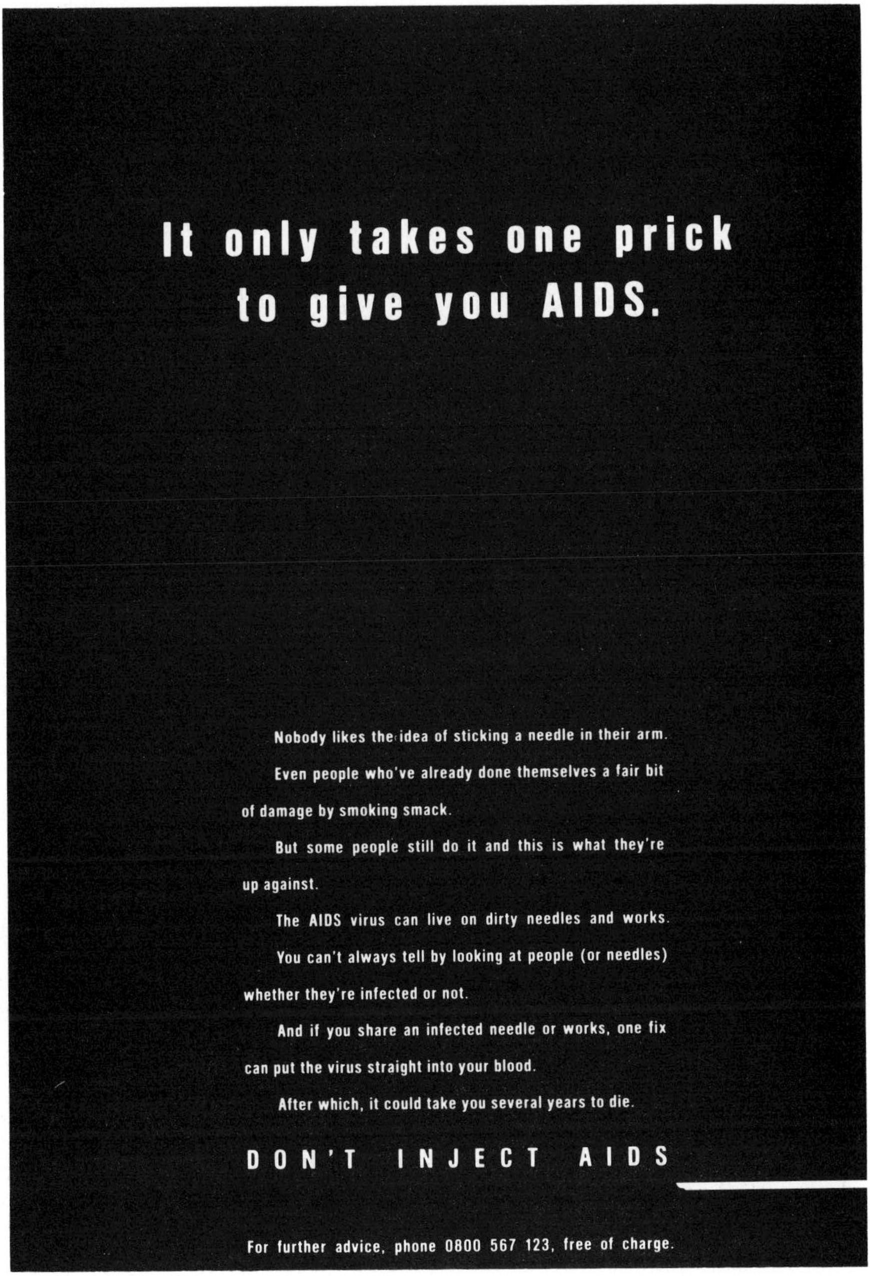

Figure 4 Focusing the target group

issue, the campaign took another shift and in 1988 the strategy was changed to focus on young, sexually active heterosexuals.

THE HEALTH EDUCATION AUTHORITY

In 1988, it was decided that the campaign should be taken over by the Health Education Authority (HEA), an independent body funded by the Government. TBWA produced two highly success-ful TV advertisements for the HEA based on the brief of improving recognition on the dangers of casual sex. The first, 'Coffee', shows a girl asking a boy back to her flat for a drink. The ad is overtly soft and erotic in style, but is counterpointed by captions warning of the dangers of AIDS. It is the deliberate pastiche of romantic films that makes the film memorable; and remembered it was. Throughout March and April 1988, the ad was at the top of *Marketing* magazine's top twenty recalled advertisements. The second film, set in a disco, works less well, but the ads are important primarily because they personalise the message.

In spite of extensive research, which showed the benefits of using mass media to communicate the dangers of AIDS, after 'coffee' and 'disco', the HEA decided to focus their efforts on local education. The tight team, which had been fundamentally impor-tant to the rapid development of the advertising, was lost, as was the approach of marketing the advertising, to the media to try to expand the impact of the campaign. However, after a lull, the HEA returned with its new agency, BMP DDB, to mainstream press, cinema and TV work with personalised and even humorous work such as Mr Brewster (80), who with his re-usable condom, encourages people to practise safe sex.

THE EFFECTS OF THE CAMPAIGN

AIDS has not yet turned into an epidemic in the UK, but there were over 6,000 AIDS cases identified between 1982 and 1992. This and the future development of the disease are the ultimate tests of the effectiveness of the government's public education campaign. The first campaign, featuring the iceberg and the monolith, was undoubtedly successful in meeting the objective of raising aware-ness of AIDS among the general population. The campaign to link drugs with AIDS seems to have been successful in reducing the appeal of drugs, although the caveat should be added, that it may also have had the side-effect of de-identifying large sections of the population with AIDS. Finally, the personalisation of the message to young heterosexuals seems to have worked in terms of understanding of the disease. What is notable, however, about this body of advertising is the lack of consistency of style and approach. With AIDS advertising, there has been a series of short campaigns. Primarily, this has been due to the variety of messages and target audiences, but also there has been a rapid change in attitudes and opinions. Sammy Harari says:

> When you look at sixties and seventies advertising, it looks so dated, because over a five- to ten-year period attitudes and fashions change. What characterised AIDS advertising was that change literally happened over a six-month period. And therefore the advertising, which might have been right at a particular point in time, rapidly became outmoded.

However successful the AIDS campaigns have been in promoting awareness and changing attitudes, the important issue in the fight against AIDS is the effect on behaviour. Part of the role advertising can play is to help speed up behavioural change. Was this achieved? Certainly, sales of condoms have gone up dramatically (+50 per cent, since 1985) and some people are practising safe sex and reducing their number of partners. However, some of the evidence that has come through from hospitals, such as St Thomas's in London, suggests that it tends to be the wrong people who are often frightened enough by the advertising to have AIDS tests and who have started purchasing condoms. These are the less sexually promiscuous and consequently less at risk. The available research does not therefore provide any definitive answers and the role advertising has played in actually changing behaviour is almost impossible to identify.

The spread of AIDS so far has remained confined primarily to the high risk groups, but there is still the possibility that AIDS will spread into lower risk sectors of the population. If it does, then we may see more broadly based communications again. Certainly, the scale and impact of the AIDS campaign, even if it has seemed to lack a clear long-term strategy, has been the most significant public education programme ever in the UK and, compared to action taken elsewhere in the world, has been thoroughly comprehensive. However, relative to money spent on advertising Government privatisations, the sums have been small and there is an argument for suggesting that in the long term, changing behaviour can only be really effected by changing moral attitudes — a bigger and broader task altogether.

Points to Note

- Social persuasion advertising needs to be finely tuned. In most cases you are asking people to do something they don't want to do. Therefore the motivational triggers need to be right to get people to respond to a message, rather than turning away from it.

- Most of the AIDS advertising achieved the targets specifically set. However, viewed as a whole the work is dissonant. This is due to the different requirements of target markets, the changes in personnel and structure and the lack of a long-term advertising strategy — an inevitability, given the rapid change in attitudes among the population.

- The campaigns (using mass media) were highly effective in raising awareness and changing attitudes, but the effect on changing behaviour is much disputed.

- The AIDS campaign rapidly changed the level of explicitness most people were prepared to accept from advertising.

7

RCA CONSUMER ELECTRONICS

MAKING THE MOST OF YOUR HERITAGE

CHANGING ENTERTAINMENT. AGAIN.

As well as being an early film producer and record company, Radio Corporation of America (RCA) were the inventors of television on a commercial basis. This gave the company an early advantage in penetrating the vast US market for television sets which burgeoned after the Second World War. For forty years RCA sets dominated the market and the living rooms of America. However, like many early innovators, the company enjoyed such success that it ceased to think about innovation. As the consumer electronics market exploded in size and diversity in the seventies and eighties, RCA began to be left behind. By the late eighties, it was still the market leader in colour television sets, but there were new products, such as video cassette recorders and camcorders and new, young and affluent consumers, where RCA was failing to make an impact. When the French electronics group Thomson acquired the company from the General Electric Company in 1987, it recognised that the RCA brand needed to be revitalised. Japanese competitors, such as Sony, Sharp, Toshiba and Panasonic, had entered the market with well-designed, high technology products and were eating into RCA's market share on all fronts. If nothing was done, RCA would be left with an ageing consumer profile and product range. Thomson decided to look at the way the product was advertised and asked a number of agencies to pitch for the business. One of the agencies was Ammirati & Puris.

THE MARKET BACKGROUND

Part of the problem that RCA faced was to do with its heritage. Having become such a well-established brand in the US, it was very familiar to consumers and consequently was tainted by associations with ornate, wooden cabinets in grandparents' homes. Of course, as Sony itself had proved (Sony America had been established since 1960), longevity in the market did not necessarily lead to these associations if the product itself was continually enhanced. But RCA was a manufacturing led company producing low technology, large-scale, mid-range television sets for the mass market; staple products that, in fact, had changed little in styling since the fifties. The heritage issue was borne out by research, which looked at the awareness of different consumer segments. RCA, as expected, dominated share of mind in the older segment of the market, who were simply looking for basic products, but in the younger 'videophiles' segment, where consumers were knowledgeable about and interested in product features, RCA had no presence. Of course, RCA could concentrate only on the basic segment, but Ammirati & Puris recognised that the videophiles were the people who were more valuable both in terms of consumer electronics sales and also in terms of influence in the market place. Also, looking to the longer term future, this younger segment would grow up with a predisposition to buy Japanese. RCA's customers would, quite literally, die. Vivian Young, Director of Strategic Planning at Ammirati & Puris, says:

> RCA shared all of their research with us. We used the research to effectively illustrate their weak position with the under-40 market makers.

The lack of presence with the videophile sector was exacerbated by the lack of advertising support for the brand. Important competitors, such as Sony and Philips' Magnavox brand, were increasing their advertising spends significantly and had seen as a consequence major leaps in awareness. RCA's share of voice had decreased by some 33 per cent and their share of mind was static. This created a vicious cycle, aggravated by retailers discounting prices, which reduced margins and squeezed advertising budgets; whereas the competition had advertising to sales ratios of 2 per cent to 3 per cent, RCA's was 0.6 per cent.

RCA's previous failure to innovate had also encouraged retailers to ignore the brand. It was on the shop floor and it sold to a certain type of customer, but the Japanese kept providing exciting products which gave salespeople the opportunity to sell something new to consumers who were interested in technology and features (even if they subsequently never used the features that had led them to buy the product). Inevitably, when RCA tried to introduce new ideas, such as a wide-screen format TV, research showed that consumers did not associate such a product with RCA and didn't believe that RCA was capable of bringing it to the market.

The advertising challenge was therefore considerable. There was a need to overcome a severe image handicap, maintain market share with a traditional market segment while appealing to a new one, and create retailer interest — all on an initial budget of $10 million.

THE ADVERTISING CHALLENGE

One of the advertising options open to RCA was to try to compete head-on against the Japanese; to use technology and features to get consumers to re-appraise the brand. However, RCA did not really have the products to compete on a technological basis, as defined by the Japanese. Nor did Americans necessarily want more technology *per se*. TV programmes such as *The Tonight Show* and *Saturday Night Live* lampooned the complexity of VCRs and the inability of consumers to actually use them. RCA decided to concentrate on technological innovation that would make the products easier to use; and in a move away from the wooden box set, they invested $300 million in research and development to enhance both the usage and the styling of their products.

Ammirati & Puris decided to develop a campaign that would reposition RCA by using its heritage as an entertainment provider. This would help ensure that RCA stood out against the competition and also reassure the traditional customer base about the constancy of the RCA product. But would it meet the other objectives of:

● re-vamping the brand image amongst a younger target market;

- creating visibility for TVs and a new range of camcorders, VCRs and large screen TVs;

- inspiring trade support?

The answer was to balance the heritage message with a sense of change. Creatively, the answer was to re-introduce 'Nipper', the dog who, while listening to his master's voice, had been a symbol for the company for over 100 years and had first been used in advertising in 1929. Not only was he the antithesis of the technological approach, but he was also well recognised as a branding device. The existing high awareness of Nipper would thus help overcome the constraints of limited budgets. The element of change would be suggested by giving Nipper a son; an eternally young puppy who would represent the new, forward-looking RCA. The route was not as obvious as perhaps it seems. Mary Herrmann, Executive Vice-President of Ammirati & Puris, explains:

> We started the creative process using an updated Nipper alone. But we found that, no matter what the context was, consumers still attached warm, but old-fashioned, imagery to him. Adding the puppy, Chipper, worked like magic.
>
> Consumers easily attached perceptions of 'new' and 'state of the art' to the pup and felt comfortable and reassured with Nipper. The dual symbol achieved the perfect image balance for the new RCA.

The balance of new and old was also emphasised by developing a brand statement to appear on all communications: 'Changing Entertainment. Again' makes the point about change and heritage. It also stresses the benefit of RCA products providing entertainment, not boxes of technology. Having got the basic elements of the campaign worked out, the next task was to determine how they would be used.

THE CREATIVE IDEA

The whole focus of the creative approach was to stress the consumer benefits of RCA's technology. This meant showing the range of products and what they could do. The ad that best sums up the idea is 'At last, technology that serves man', which features a simple touch, remote control that only has the six most commonly used buttons, a sound retrieval system which provides stereo sound without having to hook up speakers, and an easy-to-use VCR (Figure 1). The technology is balanced by the dogs, who not only grab attention, but inject humour and warmth. The message to be taken out of the ad is that RCA is a brand whose complete orientation is towards the consumer.

When it came to TV executions, the same balance of technology and humour was continued. Practically, this was not always easy to achieve, when trying to train a two-month old Jack Russell puppy, with a short attention span, to press a remote control. Nonetheless, by filming short sequences and using four different puppies made up to look the same, a series of 30 second TV films was made using the dogs to demonstrate the ease of use of various products. RCA's large-screen TVs, which the company branded under the name of Home Theatre, were presented in a series of spots, all of which make the point that the screen image is so real that it interacts with the viewer — an idea that Woody Allen explored in the *Purple Rose of Cairo*. One of the spots features the puppy with a sunflower in a darkened room. As the TV comes on to Johnny Nash's *I can see clearly now* with an image of a rising sun, the room is filled with shafts of sunlight and the flower, flanked by the two dogs, turns towards the TV screen (Figure 2). Another spot, which demonstrates the light weight and compactness of RCA's camcorder, has the puppy parachuting into a garden with the camera strapped to its back.

In fact, a large number of executions have been developed, with many of the early executions using different 10-second films spliced together. The rationale behind this was that with limited budgets, the ads could be re-arranged to keep grabbing the viewer's attention and also be adapted to present new product features. The downside of this is that the early work tries to communicate too much — three ideas instead of one make the films disjointed and over-complex. In comparison, the later work, such as the Johnny Nash Sunflower, are more impressive for their simplicity and singularity of message.

STRETCHING THE BUDGET

To achieve the objectives for the brand, Ammirati and RCA had to make a relatively small budget go a long way. Not only was RCA

Figure 1 The introduction of Nipper and Chipper

At last, technology that serves man.

Must a VCR be so darn impossible to program? Must a remote have seven thousand buttons? Must an instruction manual be dry as the Sahara? Nay. Not anymore. We introduce a new line of VCRs that make recording a show easy as watching one. We introduce the Simple Touch™ remote control with only six buttons, for the stuff you really need 99% of

Our new line of VCRs makes recording a show as easy as watching one.

SRS (Sound Retrieval System) gives you stereo sound without hooking up stereo speakers.

The 35" RCA Home Theatre™ has Pix-in-Pix capability, a VHP picture tube, zoom and pan feature, Comb filter, and Sound Retrieval System.

The Simple Plus™ remote controls basic VCR functions.

The Simple Touch™ remote has only six buttons.

Our 24-hour hotline is toll-free.

the time. We introduce SRS (•)' [Sound Retrieval System], which surrounds you with sound without stringing extra wires or speakers. We bring you easy-to-read instruction manuals that you might actually read. And we even have a toll-free hot line [1-800-336-1900] to help you find the RCA dealer nearest you. Does it get any easier? If so, we're working on it.

RCN
Changing Entertainment. Again.™

RC/I

"RISING SUN" :30

(VIDEO: CHIPPER HITS REMOTE)

(MUSIC BEGINS: "I CAN SEE CLEARLY NOW")

(VIDEO: FLOWER BEGINS TO RISE)

VO: Presenting the RCA 52" projection screen Home Theatre. It's bigger and brighter...

...than almost anything out there.

Figure 2 Branding home theatre

being out-spent by the competition in specific product areas such as camcorders, where Sony's share of voice was 42 per cent compared with RCA's 10 per cent, and colour TVs, where Magnavox's share of voice was 32 per cent and RCA's was again 10 per cent but the competition all had other opportunities to communicate their brand values to the core target market both in advertising and in-store. Whilst RCA only compete in video products, Sharp and Toshiba also make computers and Sony make audio systems.

Two inventive ideas helped RCA to overcome these disadvantages. First, in an attempt to create media and retailer interest, a competition was launched under the 'Name that Pup' banner. As well as creating news, everyone felt it was important that consumers quickly understood the reason for creating the puppy character. The five insertions that appeared in the press, announcing the competition, garnered 81,000 entries. More importantly, editorial interest was created both in the press, in such publications as *USA Today*, and on TV, in programmes such as *Good Morning America*. Ammirati & Puris estimated that the additional coverage was worth $840,000 in broadcast and media print weight. The chosen solution of 'Chipper' may not be particularly innovative, but it rhymes with Nipper and has some connotations of technology. At least it seems more appropriate than 'Audie O'Video', 'Entertain-Mutt' and 'Paws Button'.

Second, with $10 million to spend on media, there was no real possibility of achieving the campaign objectives using prime time network TV. Ammirati & Puris believed the budget needed to be concentrated in an appropriate area. What they found was a TV producer with a concept borrowed from Japanese television. The idea was to produce a programme called *America's Funniest Home Videos*, which would simply use entertaining videos sent in by viewers — an exercise in self-humiliation. RCA would sponsor the show and all the prizes for the best videos each week would be RCA products. This provided RCA with exclusivity — no other consumer electronics company was going to advertise in the programme breaks when RCA camcorders were being given away. Ammirati & Puris then offered the TV network the whole media budget in return for one spot in every show all year. The gamble paid off. The content of the show was appropriate to the products, the type of videos sent in often had the same warmth and humour as the Nipper films, and the programme was hugely successful. The only negative, and part of the rationale for the large number of Nipper films, was that to keep the interest of the regular audience, there had to be a variety of RCA advertisements.

THE RESULTS

The Nipper advertising has so far shown remarkable versatility and in its first year (1991) has already moved a long way towards achieving the objectives set.

1. *Re-vamp the Image of RCA*
   Communications tests carried out on behalf of RCA showed that:
   — Three out of four viewers claim their opinion of RCA improved after viewing only one commercial.
   — Dramatic inroads were made towards reversing RCA's entrenched imagery. Image dimensions such as 'Grandma/Grandpa' showed a decrease of 20 percentage points; 'traditional' was down 11 percentage points, whilst the positives such as 'Among the first to try new things' was up 23 percentage points,' 'Active/on the go' was up 15 percentage points and 'Innovative' was up 7 percentage points.
   — This pattern was also evident among the all important young opinion leaders: the videophiles. Opinions of RCA improved among this group by 12 percentage points, while ratings such as 'Traditional' and 'Grandma/Grandpa' declined 25 percentage points and 17 percentage points respectively. 'First to try new things' increased by 19 percentage points.
   — In terms of purchase consideration, tracking results showed that during the first six months of the campaign, RCA significantly increased its lead over the competition for top brand considered for future purchase.

2. *Create Visibility and Voice*
   — In spite of being outspent by the competition, tracking results showed that during the first six months of the campaign awareness jumped 14 percentage points — increasing RCA's lead on the competition.
   — Post-production communications tests demonstrated that the Nipper campaign not only clearly conveys the benefits of specific product features, but does so in a compelling way.

3. *Inspire Trade Support*

Retailers and dealers in an independent, voluntary effort rallied behind the Nipper campaign and invested some $10 – $15 million in locally branded radio and TV campaigns.

As a result of the success of the Nipper campaign, Thomson has now allocated more than $30 million for national advertising. The increase in spend is because, as Martin Holleran, Thomson's Executive Vice-President of Marketing and Sales, NA, says, 'Consumer research shows that the Nipper-Chipper combination is "doing exactly what we hoped" to market RCA's products.'[1] The long-term test will be whether Ammirati & Puris can continue to develop the campaign and, more importantly, whether RCA can continue to develop the design and technology of their product range.

Points to Note

- Ammirati & Puris's advertising used RCA's heritage to position it as an entertainment provider, rather than a high technology company.

- The products and the advertising are both consumer driven.

- The creative approach in blending old and new has helped RCA retain its traditional target market, while building a new reputation with younger,influential consumers.

- The limitations of budget were overcome by a creative approach to media and promotions.

Reference

[1] 'RCA Stresses ease of Use in Electronics Campaign', *New York Times*, 25 September 1991

8

HARVEY NICHOLS

© **HARVEY NICHOLS**

THE RETAILER AS A BRAND

The way in which our perception of a company or a brand is formed varies, depending on the product and how we use it. In the first case in this book, it was shown that consumer perceptions of Absolut Vodka were formed primarily by advertising — the product itself being indistinguishable from other vodkas. However, with a retailer, perceptions are dominated by the physical experience of visiting a store. For example, British consumers have a very clear perception of Marks and Spencer because they regularly shop there, not because of the company's advertising — historically M & S have advertised very little. What then is the role of retail advertising? Traditionally it has been twofold. First, it has been to increase immediate footfall, ie the number of people visiting the store, by advertising specific prices, limited offers, promotions and sale events. Second, it has been to build a perception of the retailer as a brand. Most retailers are far better at the former than the latter. However, a retailer such as the fashion store Harvey Nichols, which trades on the strength of its designer ranges, has to be adept at brand building.

BACKGROUND

Harvey Nichols is hard to describe. It is not a department store in the way that Harrods is; nor is it just a clothing store. It sells both womenswear and home furnishings and food. What seems to unify it is its emphasis on fashion and style. Since the turn of the century, Harvey Nichols has sold from its Knightsbridge location the best brand names to the rich and the famous and the royal. Although one is wary of describing it as such, it has become an institution.

Unfortunately, like many British institutions, it has languished in recent years. Having had only three owners since its foundation by Benjamin Harvey in 1813, in 1985 the shop ended up in the hands of the Burton Group — a broadly based clothing retailer. Although Burton ran the shop successfully for a while and revived its fashionable status, they were never able to make much money out of it. By 1990, Burton had hit problems of its own, caused by the onset of recession and its exposure to the fast declining property market. To reduce debts, Burton began to look to off-load their portfolio of retailers. When Dickson Poon, a Hong Kong based businessman, offered £60 million for the store, Burton readily agreed.

DEVELOPING AN ADVERTISING STRATEGY

Dickson Poon's companies have a common credo: conservative on accounting, aggressive on marketing. Consequently, one of his first initiatives was to review the role of advertising. Traditional fashion advertising was dominated not by the retailers, but by the designers and the power of the magazines. This had meant that in the past Harvey Nichols had done two types of advertising:

- *Advertorials* — where magazines like *Harpers and Queen* and *Vogue* would launch promotional themes, such as women travelling abroad in autumn. Eight pages would be devoted to the theme and Harvey Nichols clothes would be featured in return for an acknowledgement.

- *Designer ads* — where, for example, Harvey Nichols would contribute to an ad for the American designer, Donna Karan. This would gain an acknowledgement, saying the clothes were available at Harvey Nichols.

In neither case was Harvey Nichols controlling the imagery with which it was being associated, nor was it giving any reason for a consumer to buy Cerruti or Calvin Klein from Harvey Nichols as opposed to anywhere else — Harvey Nichols was acting like a distributor, not a brand. Dickson Poon wanted Harvey Nichols to be *the* brand for fashion. Harvey Nichols decided it needed a new direction and a new agency.

HARARI PAGE AND THE IDEA OF COPYRIGHT

One of the agencies briefed to come up with a new approach was the year-old agency Harari Page. To make best use of the budget, they recognised that Harvey Nichols had to get rid of the advertorial approach and focus all their money on enhancing the image of the store. But what did Harvey Nichols have that no other shop could offer ? In spite of the replacement of 1980s designer consumerism with 1990s egalitarianism and lycra, what made Harvey Nichols distinctive was its range of designer brands. Although many luxury brand advertisers were beginning to tone down the status message at this time, if the advertising was to be true to the ethos of the store, the designers had to be the basis of the advertising. To capitalise on the diversity of the names it stocked, the creative brief stressed the need for a large variety of designer images.

The solution that creative director Alan Page arrived at was to make Harvey Nichols the central proposition of the advertising by inverting the designer ad. Now, rather than Donna Karan at Harvey Nichols, it would be Harvey Nichols by Donna Karan. Although this seemed a simple and neat idea, everyone felt that the linking word 'by' didn't read very well — what did it mean ? The 'by' was replaced by a '© copyright', which was more flexible and communicated the theme better. The second problem was that the idea relied on the co-operation of the designers, who would now find their names relegated below Harvey Nichols. If they refused to fund the ads, the idea would be dead before it started. However, because everyone at the store, including Dickson Poon, was so supportive of the campaign idea, a bullish line was taken with designers. If anyone didn't want to be involved in the campaign, then Harvey Nichols wouldn't work with them. Although there was some initial resentment, Harvey Nichols used its muscle and, with the notable exception of Ralph Lauren, the designers started to fall into line.

THE CAMPAIGN STRUCTURE

The campaign with which Harari Page won the account was based on communicating diversity through a profusion of images, and consistency through a common style and language. Partly this was

Risk vertigo.

Take our escalator all the way up to 4.

*And feast your eyes on the
most stylish home
furnishings floor in London.*

*We have exclusive home collections from
Ralph Lauren and Mulberry.*

*Plus Thomas Goode,
Global Village, Oriental Carpets,
Smythson's, Kenneth Turner, Wilson & Gough,
Belinda Coote, Nina Campbell,
Bougies La Francaise,
Besselink & Jones and Henry's.*

*So as well as furnishing you
with a fashionable wardrobe,
we can now dress up your home too.*

HARVEY NICHOLS, KNIGHTSBRIDGE,
LONDON. 071 235 5000.

HARVEY NICHOLS

© Horst P. Horst 1992

Figure 1 Harvey Nichols © Horst P. Horst

HARVEY NICHOLS

© *Linda McCartney 1992*

*Is the state
of your wardrobe
becoming something of
a prickly subject?*

*Ride on down
to our Lower Ground, then.*

*You'll find we've rounded
up the very best menswear
collections from Armani
right through to Zegna.*

*Compared to our
department, in fact,
the rest of London
is little more than
a desert.*

HARVEY NICHOLS, KNIGHTSBRIDGE,
LONDON. 071 235 5000.

Figure 2 Harvey Nichols © Linda McCartney

HARVEY NICHOLS

© *Michael Kors 1992*

A Kors celebre from
Harvey Nichols:

We so believe in this New York
designer's sophisticated and
sexy "essentials,"
that we're flying in more and more of his
wonderful collection.

You'll find it on 1 at Harvey Nichols.

(And, occasionally, on Virgin's Upper Class seats.)

HARVEY NICHOLS, KNIGHTSBRIDGE,
LONDON. 071 235 5000.

Figure 3 Harvey Nichols © Michael Kors

HARVEY NICHOLS

© *Montana 1992*

*You don't need a sharp eye
or indeed Claude Montana's
own pet Shar-Pei to recognise that
this designer is one of the few
true originals.*

*For many his clothes are
as near to perfection as one can get.*

*(Hopefully you also see our store
in a similar light.)*

*So, if you need an excuse
to take the dog for a little walk,
stroll round to Knightsbridge now.*

His master's latest collection is on 1.

HARVEY NICHOLS, KNIGHTSBRIDGE,
LONDON. 071 235 5000.

Figure 4 Harvey Nichols © Montana

because the core audience for the launch campaign was the regular Harvey Nichols shopper, who was a reader of the key titles: *Vogue, Tatler, Harpers and Queen*. With the high duplication in readership of the magazines, the ads needed to be recognised as Harvey Nichols, but the images would become repetitive if there was insufficient variety. Partly it was to ensure the advertising reflected the nature of the store itself, which had a great diversity of designer names, within a consistent environment.

To create the necessary level of consistency in the design of the ads and thus ensure they were always immediately recognisable, Harari Page developed a structure to the campaign. First, all advertising would be double-page spreads. The left-hand page would always feature Harvey Nichols branding, with the designer's copyright and a small nugget of stylish, witty, copy explaining either the background to the right-hand page or making a more general point about Harvey Nichols. Second, the right-hand page itself would feature one of three types of image:

1. *Generic*: an image that would be bought or licensed from a famous photographer. The images have all been old black and white shots, mostly from the golden age of fashion, by photographers, such as Horst P. Horst and David Bailey. The aim is to get consumers to associate the style that can be found in the photographs with the style on offer at Harvey Nichols. Thus Horst's shot of an interior (figure 1), which appeared in *House and Garden* in 1952, was used to launch the home furnishing floor at Harvey Nichols in 1992. These generic images, which are paid for by Harvey Nichols rather than suppliers, are used to launch new collections or events or floors.

The same idea has been applied to men's fashion, but because the male target market is younger and driven more by contemporary images, the chosen photographs are more recent. Hence the use of Linda McCartney's work (Figure 2) to launch the menswear collection in 1992.

2. *Designer*: paid for by the designer and reflecting their style. As Paul Nathan of Harari Page says:

> This right-hand page is the designer's canvas — what we want to do is pick up on the essence of the designer.

Although as much input as possible is sought from the designer,

Harari Page have creative control over the final product. For example, when US designer Michael Kors was invited to participate in the campaign, he suggested shooting Yasmin LeBon on a plane. However, the style and the pose were art directed by Harari Page (figure 3). The final shot always tries to reflect the style of the designer, even when that results in a radical image. Claude Montana, the French avant-garde designer, had a picture of his Shar Pei dog, which he wanted to dye blue — his house colour; Harari Page added the silver dog bowl with 'Harvey' written on it (figure 4). Rifat Ozbek, who was recently named British Designer of the Year, has been using American Indian themes, so a photograph of a feather was commissioned as an expression of this. For Cerruti, who designed and made the clothes for Fellini's *La Dolce Vita*, the image features the 1960 film poster.

3. *Co-op*: utilising a designer's existing image. For example, Donna Karan, who is the career woman's designer, has an advertising image that has been used in the US, but not in the UK. Harvey Nichols borrowed the image, but put it within the framework of the Harvey Nichols design. Similarly, French fashion house Georges Rech had a selection of fashion shots taken, which Harari Page put on a lightbox and photographed.

The three types of advertisement are then rotated across the media schedule depending on the time of year and the need to balance generalised statements about Harvey Nichols with specific designer images. Although the generalised, generic ads do have some longevity, the designer ads tend towards the ephemeral and normally appear once or twice. The consequence of this is a slightly higher than average production budget — although the creative profile of the campaign is such that photographers and artists want to work on it and will consequently reduce rates.

TARGET MARKETS AND MEDIA STRATEGY

When Harari Page were awarded the account in November 1991, there were immediate time constraints. To launch the new season, ads had to start appearing in the key titles in March, which meant supplying copy to the publications in January. The first two ads to be developed featured a black and white photograph by Elliott Erwitt and a designer ad featuring a dress by Jasper Conran (figure 5). Initially, to get the campaign going, the ads appeared in the core

HARVEY NICHOLS

© *Jasper Conran 1992*

Fashion shows or west end shows,
Jasper Conran
always shows a sure touch.

Here he defines the appeal of Harvey Nichols. (The essentials. With a generous helping of the outrageous.)

Jasper's hat,
made by Philip Treacy, is on show nightly in
'My Fair Lady.'
His dress, daily in Our Fair Store.
So why not
poppy round a.s.a.p.

HARVEY NICHOLS, KNIGHTSBRIDGE,
LONDON. 071 235 5000.

Figure 5 Harvey Nichols © Jasper Conran

titles: *Vogue, Harpers and Queen, Tatler* and, for men, *GQ*. The ads were aimed squarely at an AB(C1) primarily female, (they out-number male shoppers three to one) audience, who were already loyal Harvey Nichols customers. Although the advertising helped to re-inforce that loyalty and ensured that women bought their Montana outfit from Harvey Nichols rather than the Montana shop, subsequent research showed the 'loyals' didn't need the advertising that much.

Where the real opportunity seemed to lie was with the occasional shopper. Although they shared with the 'loyals' a liking for the exclusivity and environment of the store, they needed to be given reasons to increase their frequency of visit. As a group, the 'occasionals' are slightly more down-market, more aspirational and less familiar with the store. They might read *Vogue*, but they also read *Marie Claire* and *Elle*. The implication of this for media planning is a broadening of the schedule to include more titles. Now the loyal shopper will glimpse the campaign rather than be the focus of it.

CONSISTENCY

With such a diversity of imagery being communicated, Harvey Nichols recognised from the outset the importance of also maintaining consistency of style. So although each ad may only appear once or twice, the campaign builds up as a whole to make a statement about Harvey Nichols. However, this is not only important within the context of print advertising, but also in other media. For example, when the Harvey Nichols summer sale was launched with TV advertising, it was agreed that it should integrate tonally with the press campaign, rather than shouting 'sale' and 'Hurry, hurry'. The film consists of a stylish single shot, which is a close-up of the body of a woman. As the camera pans up to her shoulder, we see a hand, which as it peels away reveals a tattoo saying 'Harvey Nichols Summer Sale'. Shot by photographer Terence Donovan, there is an almost complete absence of colour, apart from the tattoo. Not only was the summer sale the most successful ever, the film has also been nominated for a BAFTA (British Academy of Film and Television Arts) award.

Although Harari Page believe the campaign will continue to develop both on TV and in the press, it is now also being carried through other in-store communications, such as store guides and charge card applications. In fact everything has the campaign imprint, except the windows, which probably already deserve the accolade of being the best designed in London.

DEVELOPING THE IDENTITY

Although some commentators have questioned the positioning of Harvey Nichols as a fashion store, Dickson Poon has been unequivocal in his strategy. The British may not be as keen as the Spanish or the Italians or, indeed, the Far Eastern markets on designer brands, but there are obviously sufficient of them to fuel the successful growth of Harvey Nichols. Since the acquisition, floor space has been increased by approximately 5 per cent, but sales have increased in the midst of the recession by 23 per cent. Although it is not possible to pinpoint the effect of the advertising, consumer research into the campaign has proved it to be very popular — even if (or perhaps because) it is a bit rarified — with both loyals and occasionals . The designers, having been initially sceptical, are now keen to get involved.

The clear sense of direction the store now has is evident in the development of the food hall, which opened in November 1992, complete with own-brand products, a restaurant, café, wine shop and drinking area. Advertising for foods will adopt the same high-style approach seen for the fashion products: haute couture meets haute cuisine. Perhaps even more important for Harvey Nichols' status as a brand in its own right has been the launch of Harvey Nichols brand name products. If the Harari Page campaign has been effective in helping to endorse Harvey Nichols' position as the last bastion of style, then the Harvey Nichols name will confer added value on those products.

Points to Note

- Harvey Nichols is an example of a highly focused campaign which has helped to create a relevant brand personality.

- Although each ad is individual, there is a strong sense of unity across the range of work.

- The campaign has managed to change the rules of fashion retail advertising, by taking control away from magazines and designers and putting it in the hands of the retailer.

- The enthusiasm of photographers and designers for the campaign has helped to stretch the advertising budget.

9

BMW OF NORTH AMERICA

REDEFINING A PRODUCT CATEGORY

THE ULTIMATE DRIVING MACHINE

In 1974, BMW was a cult brand in the US. It sold some 15,000 cars through a small distributorship to German auto enthusiasts. It was undervalued and undermarketed.

In 1974 Ralph Ammirati and Martin Puris decided to set up an advertising agency in New York. Operating from an hotel room, with enough cash for just 14 days, BMW called.

BMW AG had decided to develop the huge potential for their cars in the US. That meant taking over the distributorship and investing in advertising. Although Ammirati & Puris were new and small, they had experience in advertising imported cars, having worked in the past on both Volvo and Fiat. Ammirati & Puris beat off two major agencies to win the $900,000 account. Eighteen years on, the partnership is still going strong. The advertising budgets are bigger, sales are higher, but the core strategy, albeit redirected in the light of attitudinal changes and the threat from Japan, remains the same.

THE ULTIMATE DRIVING MACHINE

When Ammirati & Puris were asked to pitch for the account, awareness of BMW was very low. Indeed most people thought BMW stood for British (not Bavarian) Motor Works. Not surprisingly, BMW sales were small, compared with the competition: Cadillac were selling about 150,000 units, Lincoln 90,000 and

Mercedes Benz 40,000. If BMW was to succeed in the US, it would have to take sales away from these marques. To test reactions to the car, Ralph Ammirati and Martin Puris took a BMW out to a country club in Westchester County and parked it next to the Cadillacs and Lincolns. Everyone who saw it hated it. They laughed at this boxlike car with a metal dashboard and gear stick coming out of the floor. Their cars had electric windows, lots of chrome and padded leather seats. The car's strong performance and thoughtful engineering was of no interest to the country club set.

Ammirati & Puris's solution was to target a younger market, — the baby boomers — who would be interested in BMW's performance heritage and wanted a car that would express their individuality and values rather than those of their Cadillac-driving parents. To appeal to this market, Ammirati & Puris recognised that they would have to determine a new, differentiated market sector that used a different language and adopted a distinctive stance that had no connection with the existing luxury market. BMW simply didn't have the cars to compete with padded leather seats and electric windows. What they did have was performance. That would be the platform. Jan Boyle, Account Director at Ammirati & Puris, describes the new category as follows:

> We used performance as the foundation to change the standards by which everyone was judging luxury cars and as the basis for an entirely new automotive category. Until that point there had never been a '*luxury sports sedan*'. Luxury cars either did their best to mimic the living room and isolate you from the driving experience or they were two-seater sports cars.

What Martin Puris called the car was 'The Ultimate Driving Machine'. a positioning that has been enduringly successful because it was:

● totally true to BMW, its philosophy and heritage;

● suited to a small, but dynamic group of individuals who were ready for an alternative;

● designed to communicate the unique benefit which BMW offered — a luxury car that provided an exhilarating driving experience.

Initially, BMW advertising appeared in print, as there were insufficient funds for TV. The early print work talked in detail about the product's technical and design strengths and was quite clearly aimed at a young enthusiast base. Ammirati & Puris called them the 'affluent activists.' However, as the campaign developed there was an obvious need to broaden the target market to achieve the brand's full sales potential. This resulted in TV advertising appearing for the first time in 1977 with an overtly performance based message. Sales began to accelerate and reached 31,439 the next year; some way behind Mercedes, but catching up fast. BMW was moving up from cult car to status symbol.

In the early 1980s, the campaign shifted tack. The performance message was still there, but research had shown that consumers were becoming increasingly concerned with such issues as quality, safety and reliability. Simultaneously, the government was responding to these concerns by introducing a whole raft of legislation on car safety. Ammirati & Puris developed a succession of advertisements which handled these issues from a BMW perspective. Print ads featured such headlines as 'Meeting the demands of society is no excuse for building a boring car' and 'BMW: the car company that hasn't been legislated into mediocrity.' Rather than treating safety in terms of how a car responds in a car crash, BMW chose to talk about active safety; the range of tests and technical innovations that enabled BMWs to avoid accidents. Typical of this work is a 1985 advertisement (Figure 1), which talks about the BMW's braking system. Alyson Henning, Senior Vice-President of Ammirati & Puris explains this flexibility of approach:

> Basically we took that idea of performance and continually tuned and refined it so that it was always relevant to what the consumer was concerned about.

The results showed through in sales, and in 1986, BMW reached a new high of 96,759 cars. However, this was the zenith of BMW's achievement. Sales began to drop away throughout the late eighties (Figure 2). The badge of success that BMW had become was being undermined by attitudinal and demographic changes and new competitors from Japan.

BMW OF NORTH AMERICA

"Luxuries Run Deep" :30

SFX: MUSIC

WOMAN: How much longer until we get there?
MAN: About twenty minutes.

SFX: TIRE BLOW-OUT.

SFX: SCREECHING TIRES.

SFX: SCREECHING TIRES.

ANNCR (VO): Anti-lock brakes. An internationally patented suspension. Uncanny control.

Conventional luxury sedans are built to survive accidents...

...the BMW 528e is built to avoid them.
WOMAN: Let's see if they're okay.

Figure 1 Selling safety the BMW way

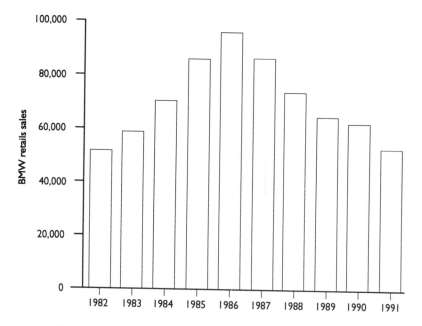

Figure 2 Retail sales of BMW in the United States

THE SECOND OPPORTUNITY

During the 1980s, Japanese manufacturers started to compete effectively in the mass car market in the US. Toyota, Nissan and Honda all successfully launched products against the indigenous car manufacturers and established reputations for high quality. Towards the end of the decade they seized the opportunity to launch luxury cars under sub-brands, such as Accura, Lexus and Infiniti. Copying the style of the German importers but providing more features at cheaper prices, combined with a strong reputation for reliability and service, the Japanese cut into BMW's market share. The US press was supportive of the new Japanese marques, and promoted the view that the car with the most features and the lowest price was the smart choice. This was a battle that was beyond BMW's resources. A five-year study of the world car industry by researchers at the Massachusetts Institute of Technology (MIT), showed that a German luxury car plant requires up to four times as many man hours as a Japanese factory in order to build a similar car. BMW simply couldn't produce cars at the same cost as the Japanese. In spite of this, for a time BMW tried to compete on features, but the results of this were largely negative and it showed through in research that:

- consumers now perceived most luxury car marques to be nearly as good as BMW;
- consumers questioned the size of the premium attached to a European heritage.[1]

Clearly, the Japanese had correctly identified a growing segment of luxury car buyers who were attracted to a high quality, low cost, luxury car. And the Japanese had the product for this segment.

BMW could not quickly change their production methods or the nature of their products. However, they could change the way the product was presented. Ammirati & Puris undertook an internal review of the business and determined that BMW could not continue pitching their products head on against the Japanese. A way had to be found, as it had been in 1974, of positioning BMW uniquely in the market. That positioning would have to be built on BMW's performance heritage, but also on an in-depth understanding of changing consumer attitudes.

NEW VALUES

A number of factors were combining to make a change in BMW advertising inevitable. The economic boom years of the late 1980s, when BMW had become a symbol of yuppiedom, were giving way to a more difficult and uncertain economic environment. Professional people were losing their jobs, stocks were down and the idea of 'conspicuous consumption' — nowhere better symbolised than by the fall of Donald Trump — was on the way out. Concurrent with this was the ageing of the baby boomers, who had been the core of the BMW market in the 1970s. As this segment entered their forties, they began to seek different values. Whereas in the past they would buy products as a means to express who they were, they were now becoming more sophisticated and advertising-literate consumers who were interested in buying products that would add value to their lives.

'A lot of the baby boomers in the 1980s were insecure consumers who used their buying binges as a way to define their identity,' said Vivian Young, the director of Strategic Services at Ammirati. 'Now, many no longer need these badges of belonging. The emphasis has shifted from the quantity of possessions to the quality of life.'[2]

This increasing consumer confidence also meant that people were less willing to pay the sort of premiums that well-known brands levied to provide customers with the reassurance of their name. IBM were beginning to experience this, as IBM clones made in the Far East moved in to take their market away. BMW were experiencing it, as new and unknown brand names such as Lexus and Infiniti began stealing their customers. People were becoming more pragmatic and looking for the best value for money. The notion held by some that customers would not buy luxury cars from the Japanese, who had no real heritage in this sector, also proved to be unfounded. BMW's target market had grown up with Japanese products and had often owned Toyotas or Hondas as their first cars. Their largely positive experiences (reinforced by positive press reports) helped create a willingness to consider a Japanese luxury car rather than a German or domestic one.

The challenge faced by Ammirati & Puris was to determine what makes an expensive car worth the money in the 1990s. Value for money and features *per se* were ruled out. What was needed was a concrete benefit that would give added value and justify the premium price and do it in a way that would express BMW's unique philosophy and heritage.

THE IDEA OF EMPOWERMENT

From conversations with BMW drivers, Ammirati & Puris arrived at an idea that set BMW apart from its rivals. Other manufacturers, such as Lexus and Mercedes and Cadillac defined luxury in terms of the drivers' isolation from the world around them — a sound-proof and feel-proof experience. BMW was a car that kept you in touch with the driving experience; it had the potential to make you a better driver; to give you control and confidence; to empower you. Apple had achieved the idea of empowerment with computers; there seemed to be no reason why BMW could not do the same with cars. Ammirati & Puris recognised that it was not going to be important to all people, but for those people who put cars high on their list of priorities, it was an undoubted opportunity. Research by DYG Scan seemed to confirm the idea:

> The more pragmatic consumer is placing more importance on experience than on the acquisition of objects. Those products which heighten experience and empower the individual to do more and do it better will have the edge.[3]

Having used research to establish that empowerment was an important issue in people's lives, the next question was 'How do you make that work for automobiles, and BMW in particular ?' In a sense, driver empowerment had always been at the heart of BMW's design philosophy in a way that was not true for the competition, and especially the Japanese. This meant that the empowerment positioning could be unique to BMW. All that was required was a new expression of it. Mike Lotito, Media Director of Ammirati, says:

> Everything BMW does is designed to make you a better driver — it's been an engineering driven company its entire life. However, they'd never verbalised what they did as making you a better driver; it was a performance automobile responding to the road and having that response come through your body. Empowerment comes out of the heart and soul of the company.

The empowerment concept did not therefore require any radical development of the advertising strategy. Performance was still the key, and the 'Ultimate Driving Machine' still worked. The shift was to communicate more overtly, not what the car is or stands for, but what it can do for you, the driver. The idea therefore was to build the advertising around the critical link between driver and the car. It was something that had come through from those interviews with BMW drivers. Typical comments were:

> A Lexus drives you — you are just another passenger. You drive a BMW and the car provides you with the feedback you need to be a good driver.
> If you can't feel the car, you will become insecure behind the wheel. Driving a BMW gives you confidence, and that makes you a better driver.
> A BMW — any BMW — possesses a strange sort of alchemy. It has the power to transform a duffer into a competent driver and a competent driver into a pro.

BMW OF NORTH AMERICA

TITLE: "SAFE DRIVER REV."
LENGTH: 30 SECONDS

COMM'L NO.: MQFF 2381
AIR DATE: 12/11/92

MALE STUDENT: There are so many times in this world where you just don't have control over your own life

and so when you get that feeling of control whether it's a car or something else

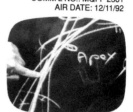

it's just a great feeling.

INSTRUCTOR: A good car gives you good information and it gives you good information all the time.

MALE STUDENT: That's quite a feeling to be able to go around a corner like that.

INSTRUCTOR: The better seat you're in the more you're feeling what the car is doing.

Does the car respond when I ask it too?

FEMALE STUDENT: This car feels like an extension of you. That to me also is the sense of safety and the sense of control.

ANNCR: A Better Driver. The Ultimate Goal of the Ultimate Driving Machine.

Figure 3 Creating a better driver

THE NEW ADVERTISING

The aim of the new strategy was to strike a chord with a broad spectrum of luxury car buyers, starting with BMW's core franchise and expanding outwards.

- *BMW's core franchise*: those who currently believe they are better drivers and therefore deserve a better car.

- *Rational aspirers*: those who feel they need to be a better driver because of rational concerns: family, safety.

- *Emotional aspirers*: those who aspire to be better drivers — and seek a symbol of accomplishment.

However, one of the things that united this audience was their sophistication as consumers of advertising. Any campaign approach would therefore have to be entirely credible. Rather than create a piece of advertising fiction which tried to disguise its motives, the solution was to produce advertising as documentary; not the clichéd in-store interview, once so beloved by some branded goods companies, but a genuine 'fly on the wall' piece of *cinéma-vérité*.

To achieve this, Ammirati & Puris recruited people from relevant demographic profiles, in much the same way as for a research study. The participants were told they would be involved in an automotive study, which would involve them in driving cars at an advanced driving school. When they arrived at the school for their induction, they were then told that the cars they would be driving for their test day would be BMWs. A documentary director was hired to record the driving sequences and also the reactions of participants. The result (figure 3) is a series of endorsements by individuals of the enjoyment and confidence that go with driving a BMW. Although competitors are not mentioned by name in the campaign, a clear contrast is made with Japanese marques, especially Lexus, who emphasise in their advertising the way external noise is virtually eliminated — an advertising idea that was first mooted in David Ogilvy's classic 'electric clock' ad for Rolls Royce. The BMW ads finish with an empowerment line: 'A Better Driver — The Ultimate Goal of The Ultimate Driving Machine.'

The $25 million, five week launch campaign started in February 1992 on network TV, supported by eight-page inserts in the *Wall*

Street Journal, USA Today and *The New York Times,* among others. It has now been developed, using the same platform, for the launch of the BMW 325i, which has again used a combination of TV and print (Figure 4). The print work, in particular, demonstrates the change of mood. The long copy ads which talk in detail about the engineering and design strengths of the car are reminiscent of Ammirati & Puris' early work for BMW, but far removed from the more style-led eighties advertising, which captured the status-conscious consumer.

THE RESULTS

The original, ultimate driving machine campaign was undoubtedly successful in raising the profile of BMW and helping to develop the brand in the US from a minority cult car to a serious contender in the luxury sedan segment. However, since the mid-1980s, when the luxury performance sector accounted for 1.4 million units a year, sales have slumped and reached 1 million in 1991. During the same period, the Japanese have driven luxury brands on to the market, causing manufacturers such as Peugeot and Rover/ Sterling to quit. Lexus, in particular, has been hugely successful and in 1991 captured a 0.9 per cent share of the US car market versus BMW's 0.7 per cent. Nonetheless, the new campaign has been widely credited with improving BMW's recent strong performance. Duncan Pollock, Executive Vice-President of Ammirati & Puris, says:

> The latest sales results for 1992 show that BMW is up 27 per cent in a market that is virtually flat.

Indeed, the three series launch has been so successful that BMW announced their intention to build a DM 1 billion plant in the US. In advertising terms, the real test will be whether the new interpretation of The Ultimate Driving Machine is as enduringly successful as the original.

THE LAW VIEWS DRIVING AS A PRIVILEGE. BMW PREFERS TO VIEW IT AS A SKILL.

In Germany, before you'd be allowed to get behind the wheel of a car like the new BMW 325i sedan, you'd first have to do a little bit of homework.

▲ At BMW, we believe that driving requires more than just a license; it requires skill. Something that a BMW, any BMW, can make the most of.

Twenty to thirty regular driving lessons, ten special driving lessons—5 on a country road, 3 on the autobahn and 2 at night. Plus twelve driving theory lessons. At a total cost of well over 1,000 dollars.

All just to obtain an ordinary driver's license.

Needless to say, in a country where there are highways that have no speed limits, they take the skill of driving seriously.

Perhaps that's why at BMW, we design our cars not simply to make the most horsepower or the most luxury, but to make the most of the driver's skill.

So while other automakers might begin the design of a new car with the proverbial clean sheet of paper, the engineers who designed the new BMW 3- Series started the process with something decidedly more important. The driver. THE HUMAN COMPONENT IS THE COMPONENT THAT MATTERS MOST.

Before any automotive component was designed, the operation of human components such as the eyes, the ears, the hands, even the feet and legs were taken into account.

The result is an automobile that acts not as a separate entity, but rather, as an extension of the driver's will.

Take the 325i's rear suspension, for example.

A design so unique it's been patented, this multi-link system increases straight-line and lane-change stability and reduces both squat and dive, while still maintaining the perfect ride-quality balance. A ride that's not so harsh as to be uncomfortable, but not so soft as to insulate the driver from the road. A BMW feature that, when combined with engine-speed-sensitive, variable-assist power steering, translates into better "feel" for the pavement traveling beneath the tires.

Which in turn translates to better control.

Which in turn leads us to the 325i's engine.
PERFORMANCE AND LOW MAINTENANCE. YOU REALLY CAN HAVE THE BEST OF BOTH WORLDS.

Perhaps one of today's few real-world examples of better living through science, the newest BMW engine features 24 valves that require no adjustments during scheduled service checks. In fact, the 189-hp M50 engine needs almost no regular maintenance beyond the routine changing of oil, filters and spark plugs.

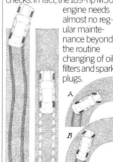

A

B

▲ In a recent Road & Track test, a BMW 535i stopped a full 10 to 40 feet shorter than any of the other sedans tested. The new 325i, of course, employs the latest-generation BMW antilock brakes, providing for control even in emergency braking situations.

▲ In a car that over-steers (A), the rear tires have a tendency to slide out of control when taking a turn. BMW's are engineered with a slight under-steer (B). This provides for a turning characteristic that is easier to control.

3-SERIES Beneath the skin of the new BMW 325i, one can find the latest in automotive technology and engineering. Technology not for the sake of technology, but technology for the sake of the one component BMW engineers refuse to design into obsolescence. The driver.

Additionally, an advanced diagnostic system has been incorporated to allow the BMW technician to "play back" past engine events, making it easy to pinpoint problems that could otherwise be difficult to detect.

But what you will truly find confidence-inspiring about this engine is that its economy of maintenance hasn't resulted in an equal economy of horsepower.

Press your right foot down. The words "low maintenance" definitely will not be the ones that come to mind.

THE 325i IMPACT-ACTIVATED SAFETY SYSTEM.

Our engineers have long contended that high-performance automobiles designed around the driver's needs are, by their very definition, the safest cars as well. And the BMW 325i

provides most compelling proof.

Unfortunately, not everyone on the road is driving a BMW. And in the event of an unavoidable accident, the 3-Series is quite ready to respond — by automatically

▲ A unique, patented design, the 325i's multi-link rear suspension increases straight-line and lane-change stability and reduces both squat and dive, while maintaining the perfect ride-quality balance.

launching an entire sequence of events designed to minimize any potential injuries.

Hydraulic bumpers absorb a portion of the impact, as do the BMW "crush tubes" they're attached to. Safety belts tighten their grip. Three sensors trigger the driver's-side airbag.

The BMW 325i sedan is engineered to offer you substantial financial protection as well.

Like all BMW's, the 325i is covered by our 4-year/50,000-mile bumper-to-bumper warranty* to reduce the risk of unexpected expenses, as well as a nationwide Roadside Assistance program you can call upon 24 hours a day, 365 days a year, from anywhere in the United States.**

For the location of the authorized BMW dealer nearest you, call 800-334-4BMW.

Because if you agree that driving is not simply a necessity, but rather a skill that should be taken seriously, you should test drive the car that takes the driver seriously.

The BMW 325i.

THE ULTIMATE DRIVING MACHINE.

© 1992 BMW of North America, Inc. The BMW trademark and logo are registered.

Figure 4 Launch of the BMW 325i

Points to Note

- BMW's original success can be attributed to defining and communicating a new automotive category: the luxury sports sedan.

- The company has maintained a consistent branding since 1974, based on 'The Ultimate Driving Machine.' This has guided the company's communications through legislative and competitive changes.

- As the market changed demographically and competitively in the late eighties, so BMW recognised the need to reposition itself in the market, just as it had done in the early 1970s.

- Driver empowerment has given BMW a clear point of difference that is relevant to consumers and appropriate for the product.

References

[1] Allison Fisher, Familiarity and Image Study, 1990; BMW High End Advertising Evaluation, 1991; Market Sense, Gallup, 1991
[2] 'As Baby Boomers Turn 40, Ammirati and BMW Adjust', *New York Times*, 26 July 1990
[3] DYG Scan, 1991

10

LEE JEANS

A RATIONAL MESSAGE WITH AN EMOTIONAL APPEAL

THE BRAND THAT FITS

> Stylish imagery always works harder when it's firmly attached to unique product qualities.[1]

Over the last 30 years, jeans have become a fashion product. This has encouraged jeans brands from Levi to Lauren to develop fashionable, stylish and often highly creative advertising. However, although many of the advertising images suggest a desirable 'must have' product, they ultimately fail because the advertising ignores the product attributes that differentiate one brand from another — a victory for style over content. Fashionability may be a prerequisite for denim brands, save those who compete on price, but the two most successful brands in the US — Levi and Lee — have used advertising not only to suggest style, but also to communicate unique qualities. Lee, which is America's number two brand, has become, partly through adversity, a highly focused brand with a relevant and clearly communicated product difference.

DISCOVERING PURPOSE THROUGH ADVERSITY

During the 1960s and 70s denim jeans were the mainstay of youth fashion. Brands such as Lee and Levi began selling their products, not as work wear but as a fashion item to 15 – 24 year olds. Levi quite specifically targeted a male audience, while Lee was more broadly based and sold more to women. Alongside the established products and brands, new colours, finishes, shapes and designer names began to appear. There seemed to be no end to the potential of the market. For example, in 1950 Levi's sales (after 100 years in business) were about $2 million. By 1975 sales had reached $1 billion. Then in the early 1980s the denim category launched into a steady decline. The main reason for this was that jeans were seen to be a youth oriented fashion market. The 'baby boom' generation which had sustained its growth was ageing and wasn't being replaced in sufficient numbers by a new jeans-wearing young, who, in any case, were less numerous and had found other fashion alternatives. Lee's initial answer to this problem was to try and re-establish denim as a fashion purchase through product innovation. If 'youth' wanted something different from the blue denim jean, Lee would give it to them. The company experimented with new finishes and styles and colours, but this failed to bring back the denim wearer and really only served to distract Lee from their core business, which was to make a basic jean. It also stretched Lee's credibility, because the product was not seen as a fashion leadership brand.

What helped to re-establish both Lee and Levi was a return to basics: Levi to its standard, male-targeted 501 brand, Lee to a female-targeted five-pocket jean. Indeed, Lee decided to promote its core product advantage: Lee cut its jeans on a curve, rather than on a straight line — the accepted way of manufacturing a denim — resulting in a better fit. One of the products manufactured in this way was the Relaxed Rider, which was cut for and specifically aimed at women. It created the opportunity for Lee to promote a unique positioning. The company decided to look for a new advertising agency to help communicate the fit message of Relaxed Rider. After a competitive review, in 1986 Lee appointed the Minneapolis based agency, Fallon McElligott.

THE BRAND THAT FITS

Although perhaps in retrospect the idea of fit as a brand proposition seems logical, it was a significant departure from the norm. First, other brands accepted fit as a given and concentrated either on developing a distinctive personality, which was communicated through lifestyle advertising, or on price-led messages. Second, Lee was targeting older women who were more likely to be motivated by the fit message. This was a generation that had grown up wearing denim, but as they were the first generation to do so there was no guarantee that they would continue to wear jeans into their thirties and forties.

Rather than suggesting, through choice of models, that what you need is a better body, the Fallon approach was to say you need better fitting jeans: 'the brand that fits'. The first TV execution took the idea of women's concern about their weight and how their clothes fit them and turned it into a problem/solution ad which showed women struggling to get into their jeans. The solution to this problem was the Lee Relaxed Rider. The campaign also extended into print, but it was to be short-lived: in 1987, a new President was appointed to VF Corporation (Lee's Parent), and the strategy was changed.

The problem for Lee was that the trade, especially at the department store end of the business, was critical of the advertising. Buyers in this sector had been brought up to buy fashion brands and here was this product called Lee that was eschewing fashion and was advertising fit instead. They felt the advertising was too old and too 'missy' and they told Lee so. Lee's interpretation of this feedback was to say that these buyers want fashion and you can't be focused on an older target market *and* be fashionable. Lee therefore redefined its target market to an 18 – 34 year old consumer and asked Fallon McElligott to produce style led advertising. The creative executions (Figure 1) show in a stylised way moments that people can identify with, especially younger women searching for identities and ways to define themselves. Fallon tested the finished work in consumer research and the lifestyle approach communicated well and was very positively received. The advertising won lots of acclaim, was popular with the trade and with the consumer. But it wasn't Lee — something the research company had also pointed out. As Fallon McElligott copywriter Bill Miller says:

> From a creative standpoint, it was really interesting work. Where it failed is that it wasn't a good match in personality for Lee. It would probably have worked better if it had been for a different brand — something a little more hip.

The work ran for two years on TV and in print. In spite of the appeal of the advertising, Lee's business got worse.

THE RETURN TO FIT

In 1989, Fallon McElligott undertook qualitative research among groups of 25–44 year old women. Fit came through as the

Figure 1 Lee's style-led advertising campaign

strongest issue. There was a lot of physical discomfort associated with wearing jeans and there was a great deal of consumer irritation about shopping for them. Most jeans were too tight in the wrong places and were definitely not cut for women, especially slightly older women whose body shapes had changed. Women wanted a product that would fit in the waist and the hip, but in which they could easily move around without being uncomfortable. This inability to find comfortable jeans was confirmed by the surprising fact that, on average, women would try on sixteen pairs of jeans before finding a pair that fit. Consequently, they tended to try on jeans whenever they were shopping, rather than making a specific shopping expedition. However, amid this irritation with fit, one brand seemed to stand out: Lee. Female consumers saw it as a superior fitting product, which was designed for them.

The research also brought out that consumers of this generation felt very emotional about their jeans and would keep pairs for years, in spite of the fact that they had gone out of style or would never fit them again. It seemed almost as if they were souvenirs of different stages in their lives and it did seem to hint that they would continue wearing jeans as they got older. Maryanne O' Brien of Fallon McElligott says:

> Women often have a real attachment to jeans because they grew up wearing denim and it serves as a reminder of that time. Wearing jeans is a symbol of their generation.

Research also showed that women looked forward to putting on their jeans — provided they fitted — when they came home from the office or when they were going out. In fact, women tended to classify their jeans in terms of occasion usage, rather than by brand. For some women, jeans were something they wore when they were dressing up, while others put on their jeans when they came home from work and relaxed. Another group saw jeans as their everyday wear. Lee seemed to be the only brand that fitted all segments. Lee's target market of 25+ women were confident consumers who felt comfortable with themselves and were able to make shopping decisions on the basis of relevance to their needs. Peter Engel, Account Management Supervisor at Fallon McElligott, explains their profile like this:

> We describe the Lee consumer as someone who doesn't look for a brand or an association to draw comfort from; they are more 'I've decided who I am.' So there is this inner security

and what Lee represents to them is a smart, safe choice — a good value brand. They're confident enough to shop in a discount store for apparel — they don't have to go to a department store for reassurance.

Armed with the research findings, Fallon recommended that Lee should go back to what they do best: make basic products for women. Peter Engel remembers:

> We said if you can win back your female consumer, your other businesses will follow. So we went back to the positioning of Lee as the brand that fits.

Nonetheless, given the emotional relationship between women and jeans, the advertising appeal could not be purely rational. Advertising would have to communicate the rational point of difference, but put it in a way that would strike a chord with women's real life situations. The research also provided the clues as to how this could be achieved. The first TV execution showed a thirtysomething woman struggling to get into various pairs of old jeans, before she tries on her pair of Lee (figure 2), which, of course, fit perfectly. Although cynically one might wonder why she didn't try those Lee jeans on first, if they always fit so well, the basic message is very effectively and stylishly put across.

Subsequent TV executions then developed the theme and showed women coming home from work and wriggling their way out of their work clothes and into their Lee jeans and also, in a more family oriented advertisement, showing women with children in a series of everyday snapshots, wearing their ever comfortable Lee jeans. The female voice-over purrs, 'The brand that fits the way you live'. Copywriter Bill Miller says that the tone 'tries, through charm and wit, to connect with women's lives.' It is warm and friendly, rather than aggressive, overtly sexual or adversarial, which is the brooding tone of most jeans advertising. Most importantly, it was appropriate to Lee jeans positioning as a staple, rather than a pure fashion brand. Bill Miller adds:

> It was almost as if those two years didn't exist. Coming back to the original work was no problem — it felt right; more honest, more down to earth, more believable, more acceptable.

Figure 2 Striking a cord with women

The TV work was also supported by a series of colour print advertisements, which appeared in a variety of women's magazines. The print work,which tends to be tonally more rational, nonetheless reflects the TV work. The headline 'Tonight, all over America, women will be slipping into something a little more comfortable' (Figure 3) is the voice-over copy from the TV execution which shows women changing into their jeans when they get home from work.The art direction of the advertisements is light and feminine, while the body copy seeks to empathise with women's lives.

MEDIA STRATEGY

Having defined a specific target market, Lee allocated some $16 million in the first year of the campaign, to reach women. Although this was significantly below Levi's spend, it was well focused. The strategy for media was to target Lee's core market: 25–44 year olds in households with two or more people and with incomes of $15,000 to $60,000. To reach this market, a combination of print and TV was utilised. However, using television against this sector was problematical. Network daytime television was bought from March through to December, with a notable uplift in August and September, when volumes are high because of 'back to school' purchases. However, August/ September is the worst time of year for TV viewership — people spend their days and early evenings outside. Consequently, very little new programming is shown by the TV networks, who instead opt for a diet of re-runs.

To try to overcome this, Fallon bought time only between 9 pm and 11.30 pm, as this would be the time that people would either be coming inside or would have put their children to bed. To make most effective use of the available funds and to protect Lee's consumer franchise, media spending was also concentrated towards the end of week, ie Wednesday to Friday, and against Lee's strongest markets. To establish where these markets were, Fallon developed a computer model that took Lee's shipping data to its distribution centres and then allocated the shipments to its customers. This not only provided a picture of regional strengths, such as the Midwest and Northeast; it also told the media planners things like Kansas City was a better market than Phoenix.

Print was used to fulfil a dual function: consumer and trade. Traditionally, retailers had 'cherry picked' the Lee product range

Tonight, all over America, women will be
slipping into something a little more comfortable.

Ahhhh. Relaxed Rider™ jeans. There's no better way to feel like yourself again. Off with your stuffy 9 to 5 work clothes and into your favorite jeans. Nobody fits your body... or the way you live... better than Lee.

R E L A X E D · R I D E R S

Lee
The brand that fits.

Figure 3 The Lee colour print camp

and often Lee had been used as a loss leader. By slimming down the range and also branding the products individually, Lee showed the retailer where the volume was most likely to be. The advertising was then used by the sales force to market the core product range and power it into the trade. Peter Engel endorses this:

> If you show the trade four ads for four products, that's what they buy.

To reach female consumers, three different print categories were defined:

- fashion — *Elle, Glamour, Vogue*

- entertainment/general interest — *People, Entertainment Weekly*

- vertical lifestyle — *Parenting, Country Living, Redbook*

The broad range ensured coverage of the target market and in order to create impact, double insertions were used. In print negotiations, the media buyers concentrated on getting an early double-page spread position for the first ad, while the second ad appeared within the fashion editorial section.

THE RESULTS

This time Lee has stayed with the strategy. The 'brand that fits' work has now been running for three years. To help carry the idea forward and maintain consumer interest, the agency has been developing new work which extends the fit message. The new executions, which first appeared on TV during the summer Olympics in Barcelona, still present fit as the main reason to buy a new pair of Lee jeans, but they do so now in a more humorous way — an indication of greater confidence with the idea.

The strength of the campaign also comes through in buying intentions and sales. Lee is number two to Levi's in the jeans market, but is the undisputed number one brand of denim for women. When female consumers are asked what brand they will buy next, four out of ten say Lee. This is a tribute to the loyalty Lee has achieved by producing jeans that fit and then communicating that message effectively to its customer base. It is also an indication of the opportunity to increase market share, if retailers stock the product and merchandise it successfully.

In terms of sales, in the category of 14+ women, Lee's volume share is up 7.6 per cent, while Levi's is down 17 per cent. However, it is in the core target age group of 25 – 44 where Lee enjoys its real growth, justifying their belief that this generation would continue to wear jeans as they got older.

Lee Jeans		**Women 25 – 44**	
	May 1990	*May 1992*	*%Change*
Market Share	15.3%	18.4%	+ 20%
Total Units	7,629,758	8,958,776	+ 17%

While Lee saw a 17 per cent increase in the number of units sold over the two year period, the denim category declined by 2 per cent. At August 1992, Lee's share reached an all-time high of 20 per cent among 25 – 44 year old women.

Points to Note

- The success of Lee jeans advertising can be attributed to the company's courage in developing credible advertising which concentrates on the brand's unique benefit.

- It is important to understand both the tangible and intangible attributes of a product and then communicate them in a relevant way.

- Lee and its agency built a platform out of an intimate understanding of the dynamics of the market and the real attitudes of a clearly defined target market.

- The 'blip' shows that it is not always easy to maintain consistent advertising in the face of competitive pressures. The period of victory of style over content demonstrates the consequences of not being true to the brand.

- The 'brand that fits' work delivers a very rational message in an emotional way, by locking into women's attitudes about wearing jeans.

Reference

[1] Chris Wilkins, 'Do Good Ads Make the Product Bad?', *Campaign*, May 92, p23

11

BARCLAYCARD

BRANDING A FINANCIAL PRODUCT

THE SPY WHO CAME IN FROM THE COLD

Financial products are notoriously easy to replicate. Whereas it may take a manufacturer six months to catch up on a technological innovation, a financial product can be copied overnight. However, if a new financial product is supported by advertising that helps to create a distinctive image, that rarity: a unique financial brand, which competitors will find hard to copy, can be created. Barclaycard, the British credit card company owned by Barclays Bank, has achieved just that.

THE MARKET FOR CREDIT CARDS

Barclaycard, the first British credit card was launched in 1966. Unlike the American Express card, which was launched four years earlier, it provided a rolling credit facility. Barclaycard was joined in the market by Access in 1973. Run by the other major British banks, Access enjoyed the advantage of having the customer base of several banks rather than just one. Not surprisingly Access quickly took over as the market leader. Throughout the seventies and eighties Barclaycard found its market share declining, but because of the overall market growth, turnover and profits were consistently upwards. The growth of the market was spurred by increasing consumer confidence which translated through into greater use of credit facilities, whilst the development of the international Visa and Mastercard networks, allowed the use of credit cards abroad. The international credentials of Barclaycard, which was linked with the Visa network were also promoted by a long running advertising campaign, featuring the globe trotting television interviewer, Alan Whicker. What

Whicker gave the brand was both credibility and memorability. The latter not least because of his much mimicked, idiosyncratic style. However, by the end of the 1980s, the credit card bonanza reached its zenith. The combination of a maturing market and the onset of recession brought about a change of attitudes towards credit. This impacted on the credit card companies in two ways. First, the overall volume of transactions started to decline. As the credit card issuers receive a percentage of each transaction from the retailer or service, this caused a drop in income. Second, cardholders had become more wary of credit and were reducing the amounts outstanding on their cards. Therefore the highly profitable funds derived from interest payments were slowing down. In 1990, Barclaycard made a loss. Remedial action was required.

DEVELOPING A NEW PRODUCT

Whilst Barclaycard was making money in a growing market, little attention was paid to the product itself. Not surprisingly, with all credit cards offering basically the same service, consumers found it difficult to differentiate between them. However, Barclaycard recognised that in a maturing, no-growth market, the way to restore profitability was to gain market share by providing a differentiated product. Barclaycard would re-position itself as the superior mass market credit card, by offering the consumer a range of additional benefits, for which an annual fee would be charged. To determine the exact nature of the product the company embarked on a research programme. It concluded the optimum product was:

- an annual fee of £8;

- a reduction in interest rate;

- free purchase protection: 100 day insurance against loss, damage or theft on any item bought from Barclaycard;

- a free International Rescue Service offering help abroad — including cash and Barclaycard delivery if the card was lost; and an

- opportunity for Barclaycard Visa holders to apply for a free Mastercard.

Inevitably there would be some fall out of card holders, because of the fee introduction. However, the research also tended to indicate that the fall out would come from the people who paid off their balances each month and the non-users — neither of which was profitable. Barclaycard set itself the objective of a return to profitability by:

1. Re-structuring the card holder base.

   — The objective was to lose less than 20 per cent of card-holders following the fee introduction and to improve the quality of the cardholder base by restricting losses to less profitable cardholders.

2. Increasing turnover.

   — The target was to achieve a turnover share of the credit card market of around 33 per cent and rising, by the end of 1992, rather than 30 per cent and falling — the existing projection.

3. Increasing new cardholders.

   — Barclaycard wanted to halt their declining share of new cardholders, and increase it from 10 per cent to 15 per cent by 1992.

The first two objectives of minimising losses and increasing turnover were linked. Research had shown that the single most common reason for keeping a credit card was usage. At a time of fee introductions, when people were cutting up their cards, any card retained was likely to get used. The task was to ensure that it wasn't Barclaycard that got cut. The new product needed to be explained to consumers. The first step was to notify all card-holders by post of the changes to the product. The second was to develop advertising that demonstrated that Barclaycard offered more than other credit cards. Whicker was too clearly associated with the old Barclaycard to be a vehicle for the new. Barclaycard wanted a new agency and after a competitive pitch, BMP DDB Needham were appointed to help launch the new product.

DEVELOPING THE NEW CAMPAIGN

BMP DDB Needham won the pitch with a creative idea known as Skyscraper. With all the new added product benefits, the strategy was based on the premise that Barclaycard was the only credit card you needed. This was dramatised by the idea of people on the top of a skyscraper cutting up all their other credit cards and scattering them to the four winds to create a New York style ticker tape parade. The voice over detailed the card's new features. The whole tone was assertive and confident. However, if evidence is needed for the failings of developing creative work for new business pitches, then you need look no further. Barclaycard and BMP thought the work answered the brief. But the work foundered, both with the ITVA (who vet television advertising) and with consumers. The ITVA's problem focused on the area of environmental pollution. Cutting up cards and then littering the streets with them was not felt to be a positive image. BMP tried to get round the problem by having the cut up cards land in a rubbish skip, but this seemed to be destroying the basis of the idea. Whether the idea could be adapted or not, however, became irrelevant when consumer reactions were assessed

Just as with Solid Fuel (Chapter 5), the rational presentation of a product can bring to the fore attendant negatives. By and large consumers do not like credit cards. On the one hand credit card companies are seen to encourage you to spend money; then with the other, they slap your wrist and charge you high interest rates. 'Skyscraper', because it presented the reason for having Barclaycard in a strictly rational way, lacked credibility with consumers and brought out the negatives. Sarah Carter, Planning Director at BMP DDB Needham, says:

> If you try and talk rationally to consumers and say this is the best credit card, you get a knee jerk reaction, and they say 'oh no you're not'. You have to overcome people's cynicism by communicating your point of difference.

The research also showed that people weren't taking in the list of product features. The ad was trying to say too much and people were not translating the features into benefits. A new approach had to be found.

Rather than ignoring the Whicker heritage, perhaps there was an opportunity to use it as a transitional device, linking the old Barclaycard with the new. Then there could be a series of films dramatising the individual benefits of the card. The idea was to show a casting session where various people were auditioning to be the new Alan Whicker. (The comedy series *Monty Python's*

Flying Circus, had produced a sketch in similar vein, where various people walked around a swimming pool, in distinctive Whicker dress, talking Whickerese). The session was completed with a new celebrity becoming the Barclaycard spokesman. Several possibilities for the new Whicker were considered, including comedians Lenny Henry, Rik Mayall and Rowan Atkinson. However Atkinson seemed by far the best fit, because consumers saw him as respectable, worldly wise and cynical — important attributes given consumer cynicism about credit cards generally. The use of humour was also important in helping to create an emotional rather than purely rational response to the advertising and the brand. Alan Ayres, Account Director at BMP, says:

> Rowan Atkinson softens the image of Barclaycard. Financial organisations tend to be seen as soulless and heartless. Rowan gives Barclaycard a personality and a friendly approachableness.

In spite of these positives, the ad foundered on the lack of awareness of Whicker mannerisms and Rowan Atkinson's reticence to work straight to camera. Atkinson's career had primarily been founded on playing characters, such as the incompetent Mr Bean and the Machiavellian Blackadder. BMP decided to create a character. Enter Latham — the Secret Agent.

Latham

There has been a whole genre of British fiction based around the Cold War and spies. John Le Carré's 'Leamas' in the *Spy Who Came in From the Cold* and 'Smiley' in *Tinker, Tailor, Soldier, Spy*, Anthony Burgess's 'Hillier' in *Tremor of Intent* and of course, Ian Fleming's 'James Bond'. Bond, who made his first appearance in *Casino Royale* in 1953 was the spy as hero. He was brave, strong, attractive and possessed of impeccable taste, as defined by the goods he consumed (Bond novels are littered with brand names). Bond's fame was extended by the series of Bond films, most notably featuring Sean Connery, made from 1962 onwards. During the sixties and seventies, Bond was a cult figure defined by and defining the times. However, with the coming of Gorbachev and perestroika, the Cold War effectively came to an end. Bond's relevance as a hero was diminished.

BMP's idea was to create a new secret agent who was firmly rooted in the spy traditions of the past, rather than the post-Cold

War realities. Latham, however, would be everything Bond was not. He would believe himself to be irresistibly attractive to women, yet women would ignore his attentions; he would possess a sense of superiority that merely translated into arrogance and pomposity; and he would have a belief in his own rightness that would inevitably lead to his continued undoing. Whereas Bond always won, Latham would always fail. However, Latham was not meant merely to be a parody of Bond. With Rowan Atkinson's input, Latham would be a character in his own right.

THE NEW CAMPAIGN

In December 1990, BMP produced the first three 60 second ads in the Latham series. All of them re-state the international credentials of Barclaycard, either overtly, as in the first ad, which features a map of the world with places that accept Barclaycard or subtly through the use of overseas locations. The first execution, known as 'Tinkerbell', is the most obviously Bond influenced, and helps to set up the secret agent theme. Latham enters a workman's tent on Westminster Bridge and pulls a lever; he descends into a large underground warehouse. At the far end is a man at a desk: Tinkerbell — a parody of Ian Fleming's 'Q'. Tinkerbell welcomes Latham, who has obviously been away from action for sometime. We quickly learn that Latham is still rooted in the old Bond style of espionage. When Tinkerbell asks Latham what he needs, he replies in a pastiche of the paraphernalia that epitomised the Bond films:

> Yes, 30 yards of dental floss garotte wire, a 12 bore pump action stapler and a 5lb bag of your finest stun potatoes. And the scuba trousers. Black. High cut.

What Tinkerbell gives him instead is a Barclaycard. Latham believes it must be a weapon of some sort and asks 'ingenious, what is it?' Latham's lack of touch with reality is confirmed when a giant map of the world appears. What he believes is the mission, is merely the places that accept Barclaycard. As Latham goes to sign the Barclaycard, the pen he selects shoots out a flame. However, this is not the latest weapon, Tinkerbell merely says 'sorry, old stock'. As Latham exits, the end line of 'It does more than you'd credit' appears.

Having set up the story of the old style spy, confronting a new world which he little understands with 'Tinkerbell', the next two ads show Latham in action. 'Cairo', which introduces Latham's sidekick Bough (played by Henry Naylor), focuses on getting across the message that when you purchase goods with Barclaycard, you get 100 days free insurance. The ad opens with the two agents walking through a middle eastern bazaar. When they spot a carpet shop, they decide to investigate. Whereas Latham insists on trying to haggle with the shop owner, Bough makes his purchase with his Barclaycard. As they leave the shop, Bough tells Latham that his carpet is insured with Barclaycard. Latham sneeringly questions what could happen to a carpet, as he unknowingly sets the end alight on a flaming beacon. As they admire a scene of the setting sun, still unaware of the burning carpet, Latham says 'Ah, smell those Tuareg camp fires...unmistakeable.' (Figure 1). In this film, and those that follow, the knowing Bough is continually put down by Latham, who pompously and obstinately continues to act like an old style spy, ignoring or under-estimating the usefulness of Barclaycard. This is cleverly conveyed in the last ad of the opening series, which is set in Moscow. Here Latham has assembled the staff of the British Embassy, including the Ambassador, who he has captured and had trussed up. Trapped in his Cold War beliefs Latham accuses the Ambassador of being a mole: he has had him photographed accepting money from a stranger and has taped a conversation about a courier. The Ambassador tells Latham that these are not the actions of a mole, but a man who has lost his Barclaycard. The strange man was providing him with emergency cash. The disbelieving Latham suddenly realises his mistake as a motorcycle messenger arrives with a replacement card. Latham tries to carry off the whole episode by thanking the Ambassador for taking part in a training exercise. 'Realism is paramount' says Latham as he bites his knuckle.

The ads were launched on television in 1991. TV was chosen to build awareness and saliency for the new Barclaycard and to help replace the Whicker associations with the brand, as quickly as possible. Activity was designed to coincide with the peak times of user activity: February/March for uplifts in 'sales' purchases; June/July for holiday/travel associated spending and November/

Figure 1 Taking in the smell of the Tuareg camp fires

December of Christmas shopping. Although there was a secondary target market of potential card holders, the real target was the eight million existing Barclaycard holders.

THE RESULTS OF THE LAUNCH CAMPAIGN

Consumers enjoyed and liked the character. He pushed credit card cynicism into the background and allowed people to believe in the superiority of the Barclaycard product. Also, by bringing out the features of the product individually and dramatising them, consumers now recognised those features as benefits. There was of course the obvious danger that Atkinson as a personality would obscure the brand, but because he was playing a character and there were real product differences to talk about, that didn't seem to be happening. Sarah Carter says:

> When ads feature a famous person, consumers normally say *they should have spent the money on cutting interest rates or improving the product, rather than wasting it on a TV ad.* With Barclaycard, they say it must have cost a lot of money, but not in a negative way; more positively, because they believe it says something about the brand. Rowan helps confer respectability.

Although, not surprisingly, the campaign took some time to build and to achieve the awareness figures of the later years of Whicker, the results were impressive. Before the first burst of Latham advertising, awareness of Barclaycard advertising was 13 per cent. By the end of 1991 it had reached 34 per cent – three times that achieved by the Whicker campaign in its first year (1982). The specific messages of the three ads also seemed to be getting through:

Base: Adults who had seen the relevant execution

	London %	Moscow %	Cairo %
World wide acceptance	67	3	2
Card replacement	--	85	--
Insurance on goods	--	--	72
Others	33	12	26
	--	--	--
	100	100	100

Source: Millward Brown 1991

The campaign was also highly appealing. It was achieving significant coverage in the National press and people enjoyed watching it. Millward Brown achieved a figure of 54 per cent on this measure versus 18 per cent for Access advertising and 15 per cent for American Express. The following quotes about the campaign are taken from qualitative research:

'They're just brilliant'
'You couldn't get up in the middle of that one.'
'They're way ahead of the others.'
'About 1000 times better than the Access ones.'
'The sort of ad where Barclaycard would gain, because people would go to work and talk about it.'

Source: Post-testing, March 1991.

The advertising was also helping to differentiate Barclaycard from Access and other cards: a key factor in developing the brand, because without a retail presence, advertising has to be the key determinant of brand image.

Barclaycard were also achieving their marketing objectives. Some cardholders were lost, because of the changes to the product, but only 7 per cent of those lost were the valuable 'interest payers'. 67 per cent were 'dormants' and 26 per cent were 'full payers'. The overall result was a much more profitable cardholder profile. Turnover was increasing and a 33.5 per cent share was achieved in October 1991 — a year ahead of schedule. This meant that for the first time since 1979, Barclaycard had overtaken Access to become the most used card. The target for achieving a 15 per cent share of new cardholders was also achieved a year ahead of schedule, whilst Access' share dropped from 23 per cent to 20 per cent. The effect of this improvement in performance was felt in terms of profits. The net loss of 1990 was transformed in the middle of the recession into a £46million profit in 1991.

TAKING THE CAMPAIGN ON

The campaign didn't stop with the original three executions. Another four have since been added. All set in international locations, the new ads have stressed and extended the communication of Barclaycard's benefits. 'Dinghy', which focuses on the

100 days free insurance, is a pared back execution featuring Latham and Bough in a dinghy awaiting a rendezvous. Talking about Latham's non-service issue Austrian binoculars, with which he is scanning the horizon, provides the opportunity to get across the fact that the insurance covers damage, loss and theft. Unfortunately for Latham, who knocks the binoculars overboard, they weren't bought with a Barclaycard. The simplicity of the idea and the lack of background action allowed 'Dinghy' to really get across the linkage between Atkinson and Barclaycard. The insurance message is developed in 'New York', which has Latham salivating over an attractive United Nations economist, who he is meant to guard (Figure 2). The two other executions, 'Snakebite' and 'Kilt' both feature an international rescue theme. They must rank as two of the most genuinely funny TV advertisements — not an end in itself, but something which makes them unmissable and able to bear repeated viewings. The Kilt story features the be-kilted Latham and Bough leaving a party. Latham takes the food off a man's plate as they walk out and then returns it when he finds he doesn't like it. When they arrive at the car park, their car is blocked in. Latham, not to be stopped by such a trifle, decides to break into the car in his way. As the police sirens go off on the car, Latham realises his mistake. The scene switches to a jail. Bough has used his Barclaycard to get an English speaking lawyer; Latham has used his influence to get the Minister of Justice to get him out. Only, the Minister is none other than the man whose plate of food Latham has pilfered. Latham is consigned to spending the night in jail with three local criminals, who stare at this man in a skirt. The final shot has Latham pulling the kilt down to cover his knees. As an end of advertising break follow up, there is an additional 10 second ad featuring Latham sitting in jail still with the criminals either side of him. Nothing is said and there is no Barclaycard branding. After a few seconds, one of the criminals places his hand on Latham's knee. Latham slaps it away as he sits looking uncomfortable.

All the new ads are strong developments of the original idea and pit the sensible new man Bough against Latham's over-bearing confidence and belief in the traditions and methods of the fictional spy.

Figure 2 Thank you Barclaycard

Latham is sent to a New York hotel to guard a United Nations economist, who has just been out shopping. As soon as he meets her and sees how attractive she is, Latham is mesmerised. In her room, she suggests taking a nap. Latham enthusiastically maps out how she can sleep on one side of the bed, whilst he sleeps on the other guarding her and the shopping. Bough tells the by now undressed Latham the shopping was purchased with Barclaycard and therefore is insured. Latham, to save face, pretends his boxer shorts are for jogging and the end sequence has Latham running outside in his underwear screaming in despair 'Thank you, Barclaycard'.

Conclusion

When Barclaycard were confronted with a maturing market and a decline in profitability, they could have opted for the soft option of trying to buy market share through a reduction in the rate of interest charged. However, they took on the much harder task of trying to establish and maintain a differentiated product. The introduction of a fee was followed by many of Barclaycard's competitors in 1991, but only Barclaycard tried to develop a real brand with added values, by creating consumer oriented benefits and then developing advertising that was enjoyable and credible. The credibility factor was particularly hard to achieve, given people's general distaste for credit cards and the companies that run them. The choice of Rowan Atkinson to play the part of the spy Latham looks to have been inspired. Not only does he confer respectability, but he also reflects in his cynicism towards life in general and Barclaycard in particular, the views of the target market. If Barclaycard and BMP DDB Needham want to continue using him, there seems to be no reason why Latham cannot maintain his popularity and effectiveness.

Points to Note

- Barclaycard reversed its fortunes by developing a consumer oriented product, which it supported with strong advertising that balanced both rational and emotional appeals.

- Rather than focusing on cost reduction in a maturing market and a recession, Barclaycard invested in its future. In contrast Access reduced its spend and suffered accordingly.

- Barclaycard shows how personalities can be used effectively: by using them sympathetically and developing their characters as part of the campaign.

- Popular advertising can help make a product desirable. This is particularly important with a brand such as Barclaycard, where there is little in the way of other opportunities to interact with consumers.

12

NIKE

COMMUNICATING A CORPORATE CULTURE

JUST DO IT

Nike is the largest sports and fitness brand in the world with a 24 per cent share of the global sports shoe market.[1] It has grown, since its early days in the 1960s, from a specialist running shoe company to domination of both the serious sports and the leisure sectors. Whereas in 1974 worldwide revenues were $4.8 million, they have now reached $3.4 billion — $6 billion is the target by 1996. A combination of continuous innovation and aggressive marketing has enabled the company to take advantage of the rapidly growing market for all things connected with fitness and health.

Nike's marketing programme has won many plaudits both for its astute signing of star endorsers (Ilie Nastase, Michael Jordan, Bo Jackson, Sergei Bubka, André Agassi) and for the creativity of its advertising. Indeed, its Portland based advertising agency, Weiden & Kennedy, was founded in 1981 with the Nike business and has developed along with the company. In many respects there seem to be cultural similarities between the agency and its client, the substance of their mutual success. Not only has Weiden & Kennedy's work been highly praised and well rewarded, the output in terms of ads produced is considerable. As many as 30 different TV executions will be produced in a year, as well as specialist press ads and also fashion oriented ads. This output reflects the diversity of Nike's product portfolio, the demands of Nike's consumers and the speed of change in the market.

IRREVERENCE JUSTIFIED

When the whole range of Nike ads is viewed together, the lack of continuity is remarkable. Each ad is a work in its own right. Where it exists, the unity in Nike's communications is created by the irreverent tone of the work and also by the authenticity of Nike's sports credentials — it's the brand the superstars wear. In fact, 'irreverence justified' was a headline written for an ad, but it has come to represent, along with the Nike line of 'Just do it', the spirit of the company. The irreverence is typical of a company that was formed by a track coach called Bill Bowerman and Phil Knight, a college runner from the University of Oregon. Like Apple Computers, Nike was an informal creation, which Phil Knight ran in its early days, while working as an accountant. In the recently published book *The Story of Nike and the Men Who Played There* one gets a picture of a company which learnt about business as it went along:

> Steered by Knight, steeped in Bowerman's principles, Blue Ribbon Sports and its successor, Nike Inc., would grow up a lot like Oregon itself, friendly but intensely private, resolute but flexible. In time, outsiders, Wall Street analysts, would peer in their window, glimpse the contradictions, the deep friendships and the raucous battles, and shake their heads. On Wall Street, companies varied, but most were as predictable as the office building that housed them. But Nike didn't have foundations, it had roots.[2]

From its early days, Nike was steeped in sports, and the people who worked for the company often came from sports backgrounds. The University heritage is also still evident. Nike do not have a corporate headquarters, as such, they have a campus. They're also an organisation quite prepared to accept confrontation and controversy. Not many organisations would have been prepared to sign up such controversial sports stars as André Agassi and Ilie Nastase or the basketball bruiser, Charles Barkley; or use a pop group with an infamous reputation, like the Red Hot Chilli Peppers, in their advertising; or even have such an impassioned director, as the black film-maker, Spike Lee, direct their ads. But Nike thrives on its anti-establishment, in-your-face style.

> 'There's a natural association between Nike and people who take risks', Mr Bedbury (Nike's Director of Advertising)

said. 'With Spike Lee comes a certain amount of risk, but we respect the passion that he has in communicating what he believes in.'[3]

On occasion the risk taking has caused problems. One ad which used the line 'Get some' had to be taken off air, because it was claimed it glamorized gang warfare, while the Reverend Jesse Jackson's black civil rights group led a boycott of Nike products for a time. However, not many organisations have managed to capitalise on changing consumer needs in the way Nike have. Nor have many managed to maintain their 'youthful enthusiasm' as they have grown and become more structured. The company has continued to be successful by balancing irreverence with very successful products for serious athletes — *justification*. What Weiden & Kennedy have been able to supply is advertising that accurately reflects that corporate culture.

ADVERTISING AS ADVERTISING

In the early days of Nike's and Weiden & Kennedy's relationship, the advertising tended to focus on the technical advantages of the products. This reflected Nike's position as the brand for serious athletes. Of course recreational runners and sportsmen and women bought the products as well, because they were comfortable and it suggested they were in the know about their particular sport. However, in the eighties the company's products moved from the running track or gym into people's (especially teenagers') everyday wardrobes, so there was a need to broaden the appeal of the advertising, without losing the serious sports heritage. Nike had to become a part of youth culture; to become the status brand in much the way Levi had.

Achieving the balance in communications between fashionability and sports performance required Nike and Weiden & Kennedy to re-think the way in which advertising worked. The breakthrough really came with a 1986 ad for the launch of Nike Air — a product which used air to cushion the sole of the foot. Rather than just use TV to get over the product's benefits, Weiden & Kennedy came up with the idea of a series of black and white clips of everyday Americans intercut with athletes wearing Nike products to the tune of the Beatles' *Revolution*. The ad captured the mood of the times and the style of the burgeoning fitness revolution. It also suggested that Nike Air was a revolution in footwear technology. Press advertising would still be used to reach the more serious athletic audience with a detailed message, but from now on, TV would be the main medium for promoting the Nike personality — the justified irreverence. Reebok, Nike's main competitor, reacted to the change by hiring the advertising agency Chiat Day, who had been Nike's agency for a while in the mid eighties. Whereas Nike's work got across style and performance — especially through its use of star endorsers — the series of ads Reebok developed stressed style over function by showing people in the street wearing the product with the caption 'Reeboks let U.B.U.'.

Where Nike's ad revolution broke new ground was the ability to exploit the power of entertainment to create a bond with an audience. In contrast to most US advertising, Nike ads are meant to be viewed as a stylish piece of communication rather than a sales pitch. The teenagers who represent the core of the target market buy Nike because it's the brand worn by their sporting heros and because the advertising reinforces the image of the brand as the style leader. For example, one of the more recent TV executions features a sporting hero, Michael Jordan (Air Jordan) and a popular TV character, Bugs Bunny (Hare Jordan). In the style of *Who Shot Roger Rabbit, Hare Jordan* mixes live action with animation. The advertisement starts with Bugs Bunny being bounced out of his subterranean bed by the thumping of basket balls above. When he goes to complain, he is set upon by four basket ball playing jocks. Using his ears as a propeller they send him flying across the court. As Bugs Bunny says 'you know this means war,' Michael Jordan appears to help his cartoon friend. A basket ball court battle ensues. (Figure 1).

It is this self-conscious parody, that suspends the viewer's imagination and says this is only a TV ad. Chris Riley, Planning Director of Weiden & Kennedy, says:

> When you show Nike and Reebok advertising to 14 and 15 year old kids, the way they talk about Reebok is, 'That's a company that is trying to target me and they're trying to do ads about sports and fitness'. The way they talk about Nike is that they say, 'Look, those guys at Nike are cool, look at the way they use their advertising money'. There's an implicit

understanding that Nike could have done traditional, marketing led advertising.

PLANNING NIKE'S ADVERTISING

Traditional, marketing led advertising would have suggested in depth analysis and research of the attitudes of the target market. However, with both Weiden & Kennedy and Nike imbued with sports, there has been an almost intuitive understanding of the market and the motivations of consumers. It is akin to the intuitive, entrepreneurial approach that Toyota used to design the highly successful Lexus. Rather than using consumer research to analyse the attitudes of potential car purchasers, Toyota sent the Japanese design team to live in Newport Beach for three months to think and act like Yuppies; to be the consumers of the car. The Weiden & Kennedy creative teams didn't need to go to these lengths because they were already runners, who bought and used sports shoes.

Although some diagnostic research has been used to define creative briefs, it is very rare for Nike to test their advertising or monitor the impact of individual executions. Even when they do, the results are sometimes ignored. Briefs can also be highly simplistic. For example, research had told Nike that sometimes you have to go back to your roots as a serious sports brand and re-inspire people. The one-word brief to the creative team was 'empowerment'. The team thought about it for a while and came up with *Instant karma* by John Lennon. The lyrics fitted the brief. A series of striking sports images were added and a new film was created and run (figure 2).

The approach is obviously high-risk. There is the opportunity to get things spectacularly wrong (and spectacularly right). But the plus is that in a market that thrives on speed of change, decisions are made quickly. Not only are there new products coming on-stream all the time, teenage imagery changes so rapidly that today's socially correct theme may be outdated tomorrow. The speed factor is also vital in determining which products to support. Nike have very good grassroots contact with retailers and indeed have their own shops called Nike Town. The benefit of this connection is that there is very rapid feedback on which

Figure 1 Hare Jordan meets Air Jordan

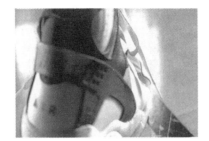

Figure 2 Empowerment through instant karma

products are selling. Nike can transfer money across sectors to support certain products when the need arises and then back into more generalised ads, such as *Instant Karma.*

GETTING THE TONE RIGHT

The traditional approach to advertising is to stress the positives of a product or service and ignore or play down the negatives. However, Nike has a positioning based on real sporting credentials aimed at 'in the know' consumers. Nike's view is that there is no benefit to be had in trying to claim that an athlete is more interesting or better than he actually is — it would easily be spotted by the expert consumer — and would have the potential to undermine the *justification.* For example, the baseball and football star Bo Jackson was signed up to promote Nike and appeared in a humorous series of ads with the theme 'Bo knows'. However, when he suffered a hip injury, which prevented him from playing, Nike decided to continue using him and have been running ads about his hip replacement. In similar vein, Nike use the basketball player, Charles Barkley in advertising. Barkley's reputation on court is as a bruiser. Rather than play this down, Nike created a TV ad which features Barkley in an aggressive animation style knocking over competitors and pulling down the basket (figure 3). What Nike is communicating is that they understand the sport; they're part of the sports world; they are the brand *of* sport.

When it comes to women's products, the tone is slightly different. Historically, Nike have lagged behind Reebok in this market. This was partly because Nike decided, when the aerobics revolution started, that it would be a fad — it wasn't; and partly because there was a concern that by advertising to women, it might undermine the product's appeal to men.

> When aerobics hit the mainstream, Nike management felt that the activity was something going on in California that wasn't a real sport...management didn't want to come off as a sissy fashion company and be in danger of losing its identity as a technical, innovative company.[4]

Having let Reebok get off to a headstart, Nike put together a

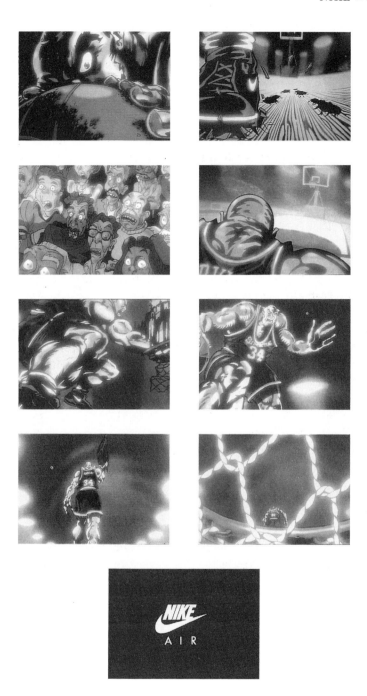

Figure 3 Charles Barkley on court

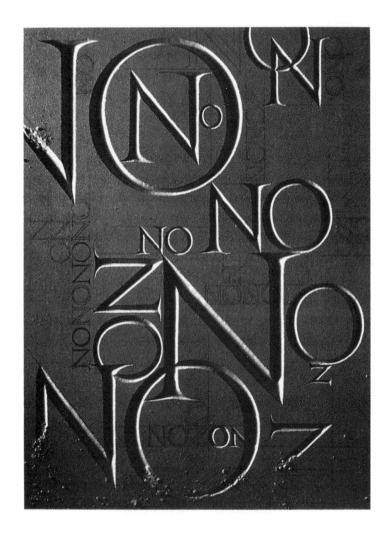

Figure 4 Women's press campaign

ALL YOUR LIFE YOU ARE TOLD THE THINGS YOU
CANNOT DO. ALL YOUR LIFE THEY WILL SAY
YOU'RE NOT GOOD ENOUGH OR STRONG
ENOUGH OR TALENTED ENOUGH, THEY'LL
SAY YOU'RE THE WRONG HEIGHT OR THE
WRONG WEIGHT OR THE WRONG TYPE TO
PLAY THIS OR BE THIS OR ACHIEVE THIS.

THEY WILL TELL YOU NO

A THOUSAND TIMES NO UNTIL ALL THE NO'S
BECOME MEANINGLESS. ALL YOUR LIFE THEY
WILL TELL YOU NO, QUITE FIRMLY AND VERY,
QUICKLY. THEY WILL TELL YOU NO. AND

YOU WILL TELL THEM YES.

strong women's range and decided that if they communicated with women as women in a personalised way, there would be no impact on their core men's market. The campaign, which was developed by Janet Champ and Charlotte Moore at Weiden & Kennedy, is an introspective look at women's lives. Using double-page, black and white spreads, the ads empathise with women and simply say: we understand the way you feel. Tonally, they are distinct from the sports campaigns, but they do have this in common: a sense of intimate dialogue between advertiser and reader (Figure 4).

Although the ads are not meant to encourage a direct response, one ad managed to jam Nike's switchboard. Women called up to say things like 'This ad has changed my life, someone has recognised how it feels to be a woman trying to get fit', and 'I'm going to buy Nike from now on because you really understand me as a woman.' The results have also been seen in sales. Nike's sales to women have been growing faster than those to men and whereas in the late eighties Nike were significantly down on Reebok in the women's market, they're currently on a par and research suggests that the brand is now more accessible and more desirable than Reebok. The campaign has also been recognised by the ad industry, winning the Magazine Publishers of America, Kelly Award for 1991 — the second time Weiden & Kennedy has won with Nike.

THE RESULTS

Brand and advertising awareness figures for Nike are consistently close to 100 per cent. This is partly as a result of the distinctiveness of the advertising and partly due to the weight of money put behind the brand. Against such measures as 'brand owned', 'brand last purchased', and 'brand you most want', Nike are consistently higher than Reebok, and on the increase. In the US, Nike has a 30 per cent share of the sports shoe market, compared with 25 per cent for Reebok. The one-time brand to beat, Adidas, has a mere 3 per cent[5]. In basketball, where Nike has a whole raft of top name endorsers — Michael Jordan, Charles Barkley, David Robinson — Nike has close to half the market. In the all-purpose cross-training market, which is Nike's second largest footwear category and single largest women's category, Nike have over three quarters of the market.

Weiden & Kennedy's work, although diverse, has helped to create a distinctive personality for the brand, which accurately reflects the anti-establishment, in-your-face culture of Nike and sustains its premium positioning in the market. That work has been consistently rewarded and as Nike's focus looks outward towards global markets, it has also become internationalised. For the first time, in 1991 Nike marketed a product with a worldwide launch and advertising campaign. To sustain their rates of growth, it is to this international market that Nike must look, and in which the advertising must work. On current evidence, the advertising is as enthusiastically received in other parts of the world as it is in the US.

Points To Note

The Nike campaign, like the company itself, breaks the rules, and succeeds: *irreverence justified*.

- As consumers have become more advertising literate, they look at advertising for what it is — a piece of communication about a company or a brand that seeks to re-inforce or change attitudes. Advertising that ignores this fact runs the risk of being ignored.

- The traditional approach to advertising is based on the premise that brand values are best built through the development of a consistent campaign theme. Nike advertising uses diversity to get across a message about itself.

- Part of the appeal of the Nike advertising is in the direct, specialist-to-specialist dialogue of the advertising. It says to the consumer who understands it, 'We're speaking the same language', and thus creates a sense of familiarity and loyalty.

- Weiden & Kennedy would argue that advertising research should be aimed at improving the quality of dialogue with the consumer, *not* with making sure you don't offend them. Research is not used as a substitute for good judgement about advertising.

- Advertising can help to build a premium position for a product by developing a relevant and desirable image. However, this image has to be sustained by product performance.

References

[1] *Sporting Goods Intelligence*, 1992
[2] JB Strasser & Laurie Beckland, *The Story of Nike and the Men Who Played There*, Harcourt Brace Jovanovich, 1991, p34
[3] Marcy Magiera, 'Spike Lee Gets in Front of Camera for Nike', *Advertising Age*, 25 May 1992, p50
[4] *The Story of Nike and the Men Who Played There*, ibid., p506
[5] *Sporting Goods Intelligence*, ibid.

13

DERWENT VALLEY FOODS (PHILEAS FOGG)

CREATING A NEW MARKET SEGMENT

MADE IN MEDOMSLEY ROAD, CONSETT

In most packaged goods markets, change is a rarity, not a rule. In Britain, where the savoury snacks market is dominated by three companies — Golden Wonder, KP and Smiths — the top ten brands from the mid-1970s are still largely the top ten brands today. This is in spite of a profusion of new brand launches and product innovations. In snacks, the well-founded truism about nine out of ten new brands failing holds true. Yet in spite of this stasis, one company has been able to develop a distinctive brand, and in so doing create a new market segment.

Derwent Valley Foods, formed in 1982, has achieved the rare distinction of successfully building a brand in a market where there are considerable barriers to entry. Both the intensity of competition and the power of the supermarket buyers make life difficult for the newcomer. However, in its favour, the company launched into a market at a time when consumer lifestyles were leading to less formal meal occasions and greater 'snacking.' It was also a market where the major players, coming from a crisps/ nuts heritage, had largely overlooked the potential for more sophisticated products aimed at adults rather then children. Backed by innovative advertising, Derwent Valley captured this market niche as its own.

DERWENT VALLEY FOODS AND THE CREATION OF PHILEAS FOGG

In the early 1980s, the British snack market was almost exclusively focused on children. Yet adults were consuming more and more snacks. Surely there was an opportunity to provide a more sophisticated product for an increasingly internationalised British palate? Derwent Valley's founders thought there was. Backed by venture capital money, they trawled the four corners of the world for product ideas, which led to the creation of four snacks: Tortilla Chips from Mexico, Corn Chips from the US, Mignons Morceaux croutons from France and Shanghai Nuts from South East Asia. Although the products would be manufactured in Britain — in a location that has now become famous — authentic recipes would be used from the country of origin. As well as authenticity, the company recognised the importance of having a brand, rather than just a series of products. The search for a name yielded 139 candidates from which 'Phileas Fogg', Jules Verne's fictional character from *Around the World in Eighty Days* was selected. Keith Gill, one of Derwent Valley's founding directors, says,

> We wanted a brand name that would convey all the different elements of the product concept: a fun, whimsical adult snack that offers international flavours.[1]

The creation of the brand name also determined the approach to packaging. Realising that initially there wasn't enough money to manufacture the product and advertise it, Derwent Valley decided to use the packs as their means of advertising until they could do the real thing. A pack was required that would ensure maximum, on-shelf prominence and tell the product story. The selected design featured Phileas Fogg in top hat, an illustration depicting the country of origin, the line 'first-class snacks from around the world' and a letter to Phileas' Aunt Agatha talking about his journey and his discoveries (Derwent Valley still receive about ten letters a week addressed to Phileas Fogg, some of which come from Aunt Agatha).

The company now had a quality product, a distinctive brand name and an impactful pack. It also believed that it had a true premium product unlike anything else on the market and that people would be prepared to pay extra for it. Research said otherwise. Trade research said the price they wanted to charge wasn't viable. But research also said that the packs should have windows, because snacks packaging always did and people liked to see the product inside. Both pieces of advice were ignored. Phileas Fogg was unique and the company had the confidence to stick to its principles. Quality was the guiding light of the company and nothing would be done to compromise that quality image, whether it be pricing or packaging.

Or, indeed, distribution: Phileas Fogg could not just be sold from corner shops; it needed listings from the dominant, large supermarket chains. The brand managed to get some test markets in the multiples and achieved sales of £200,000 in the first eight months of operation. The company wasn't making money yet, but the quirkiness of the brand name and the packaging were rapidly giving it cult status. However, Derwent Valley knew the brand had to develop rapidly if listings were to be maintained, and the fate of so many new products avoided. What Phileas Fogg needed was advertising.

THE APPOINTMENT OF BARTLE BOGLE HEGARTY

Like Derwent Valley Foods, the advertising agency Bartle Bogle Hegarty (BBH) was formed in 1982; and like Derwent Valley Foods, it set out to challenge the norms of the industry. Whereas every other agency was prepared to develop speculative creative work to win business, BBH would only offer their opinion on strategy to potential clients. Their view was that the creative work developed for pitches wasn't necessarily the best work. It made more sense to develop creative ideas, once a direction was agreed. With the reputation of John Hegarty's output to back up such a platform, some high profile clients, such as Audi, had already signed up to the BBH way of doing things. This willingness to question and to take risks made the choice of BBH appropriate to the Derwent Valley culture. Rather than asking for a competitive pitch, Derwent Valley simply appointed BBH.

Having spent their first year building up a base, Derwent Valley already had a clear idea of their market and what they wanted advertising to do. Mike Willis, the Account Director at BBH, says:

> What is interesting about them is that they are marketers in the genuine sense of the word. From the very beginning, they

had a very clear idea of their consumers and who they were. They had a whole list of attitude statements about their target market: people who enjoy exotic experiences and foreign travel, people who are willing to experiment and people who entertain at home.

Although, the idea of defining target markets by attitude rather than just demographics may be commonplace now, it was a rarity in 1983. It was also, at this stage, largely defined by market knowledge and instinct rather than research. However, when BBH subsequently used quantitative research to validate their ideas, they found that the attitude statements were right. Derwent Valley also knew that they wanted a high-profile launch, but on limited funds the money would have to be concentrated in the area with the best opportunity. This determined TV as the media and London as the region. All that was required was for BBH to come up with a distinctive creative execution.

HI-DE-HI

In addition to quantitative analysis, BBH also undertook some consumer groups to better understand buyer behaviour. This unearthed consumer pretensions about social entertaining. Although Phileas Fogg snacks were consumed by individuals in front of the television, their primary role was as party or dinner snacks. People bought Phileas Fogg as opposed to crisps because they wanted to impress their friends with their largesse and sophistication. To appeal to these people, the snob element associated with Phileas Fogg could be played upon in advertising. Pandering to people's pretensions is a well-tried route for premium products — everything from American Express (it says more about you than cash) to After Eight chocolates — but it did not seem very appropriate to Phileas Fogg. The personality of the brand as defined by the packaging was tongue in cheek and the style of the company, as defined by the founding partners, was irreverent. Mike Willis says:

Here were people who clearly took risks. They understood what the consumer wanted and were prepared to challenge the conventions of the marketplace. And that's really the spirit we took in terms of the advertising development.

Or, as Ray McGhee, Derwent Valley's Marketing Director, puts it:

We are not all things to all people. We are distinctive and innovative and exciting. There's no point in doing all the right things if you don't excite people.[2]

Rather than appealing to people's pretensions, BBH would parody them. Although BBH now seem embarrassed by the execution they developed, it did just that.

In 1983, there was a popular British TV comedy series about the employees of a 1950s holiday camp, called *Hi-de-Hi*. Part of the humour of the series was derived from the pretensions of two of the characters — a husband and wife team — who saw themselves as superior to the other employees. BBH took the two characters and put them on a cruise ship. In the ad, the suitably named Fforsythe-Jones's are about to eat dinner in the first-class dining room, where the guests are offered Phileas Fogg snacks. Although they are dressed for the part and their name 'with two Fs' has a pretence of superiority, they are not on the Captain's list of diners. They are escorted to a dimly lit bar, where everyone is singing *What shall we do with the drunken sailor?* As their drinks appear, the man offers his wife a 'pork scratching.' The end frame says 'first class snacks from around the world.'

Although this first TV execution never formed part of a campaign — it was replaced with a new style after the first year — it set two trends that have continued throughout BBH's work. First, the ad concentrates on Phileas Fogg the brand, rather than on a specific product. Even in the later executions, when there is a product story, there is always the attempt to promote the brand name and the range of products. This focus has helped Phileas Fogg always appear more substantial as a brand than its market share would necessarily warrant. In contrast, other snacks companies are more product focused and consequently relatively less well defined as brands. Second, the ad sets a self-mocking tone. We are not meant to take the Fforsythe-Jones's, nor our own pretensions, seriously. Phileas Fogg may be a first class snack served in the first-class lounge, but it's also meant to be fun. Where, perhaps 'hi-de-hi' fails is that the snobbery joke is too laboured. However, it did help to establish Phileas Fogg and in 1985 was run in a second TV region.

ANIMATION

By 1985, Derwent Valley Foods' turnover was up to £4million. There was more money in the advertising budget and a longer term campaign was required. Never frightened by the need for change, if market circumstances or objectives required it, BBH decided they could do better then the 'hi-de-hi' approach. The idea for the new campaign had literally been staring the creative team in the face. Rather than ignore the highly distinctive packaging, why not use the illustrative style and develop an animated version for television ? If the main objective was to create awareness for the brand, this route should help by drawing the pack and the advertising closer together.

It also transformed the top-hatted Phileas Fogg from a logo into a character. Drawing inspiration from the Jules Verne story, and the film that was made of it, four animated campaigns were developed showing Phileas Fogg and his travelling companion, Passepartout, sampling snacks in various exotic locations. Unlike the fictional Phileas Fogg who took no interest in his surroundings, 'being one of those Englishmen who are wont to see foreign countries through the eyes of their domestics,' the Derwent Valley Phileas takes great interest in the discovery of Java crackers (Figure 1).

He also likes to travel in style. In the second animated commercial, Phileas is trying to embark on the Orient Express at Constantinople. Unfortunately there are only places in the second-class compartment, but he bribes the guard with tortilla chips and is found a first-class berth. The original occupants retire to a smoking carriage atop the train amid the steam and smoke from the engine. The sense of superiority again comes through, as does the slightly quirky humour — something the fictional Phileas also lacked. In a presage of the next phase of the campaign, the oddity of the humour was carried a stage further in a balloon flying ad for Mignons Morceaux and Tortilla Chips, which had Phileas's and Passepartout's hats joining in a Mexican hat dance.

The four animated campaigns, still featuring the 'first-class snacks from around the world', ran for three years in two TV regions. It was undoubtedly successful in generating high levels of awareness among an ABC1 audience, and it was also able to stimulate trial of the brand. However, it had a failing, which in time both BBH

BRAND: PHILEAS FOGG
DESCRIPTION: JAVA
TIME: 00:00:00   TRANSMITTED: Saturday 1st March 1986
DURATION: 00:20 secs   REGION: LONDON   FILE REF: 86445   PAGE: 1

sound; location effects to end
male; UPON ARRIVAL AT JAVA

I MADE MY LATEST DISCOVERY

A LIGHT PRAWN DELICACY

I SHALL NAME
PHILEAS FOGG JAVA CRACKERS

LEGEND HAS IT

THEY WERE USED TO
PACIFY THE GODS

WHO CLEARLY

HAVE AN INSATIABLE APPETITE

......

PHILEAS FOGG

FIRST CLASS SNACKS

FROM AROUND THE WORLD.

Figure 1 The Englishman abroad

Figure 2 Advertising without a pack shot

WITH ONLY A
PAT BOONE RECORD

FOR COMPANY

AND ANYONE

WHO REMAINS UNMOVED

IS A HEARTLESS BOUNDER

WITH A LAUGHABLY
SMALL MOUSTACHE

....

AY AY AY

....

OH OH OH

2nd male: PAY ATTENTION
PHILEAS FOGG
AUTHENTIC SNACKS

MADE IN
MEDOMSLEY ROAD CONSETT.

and Derwent Valley recognised and decided to correct by developing the campaign again. Mike Willis says:

> I think that where that campaign (animation) was somewhat deficient was in its emotional appeal — in terms of 'this is a brand for me; this is a brand I feel passionate about'. There was a missing ingredient, which was about personality.

MEDOMSLEY ROAD, CONSETT

By 1988, the market for adult snacks had changed. Whereas in 1982 Derwent Valley had pioneered a market sector, six years later the market was awash with competitors. KP had launched a premium crisp brand called McCoys and the supermarkets had their own varieties, often made by Derwent Valley to specific recipes. The company needed to distance itself from the competition and build a relationship with its consumers. One way to achieve this was through the development of advertising that did more than say 'Phileas Fogg sell Tortilla Chips.' The ads, even if they only appealed to a limited audience, had to create an emotional link. Only then would the consumer buy Phileas Fogg Tortilla Chips, not an 'own brand' version. The question the agency had to answer was which elements of the campaign to keep and which to discard. The quirky humour had to stay, as did the suggestion of product superiority. However, the story lines based around Phileas and Passepartout could go. Phileas's very British and pompous tone would be retained only for the end frame.

Three new TV/cinema executions were created, all supposedly set overseas. The humour was influenced by the irreverent TV series *Monty Python's Flying Circus,* and is entirely absurd. The first ad was for Tortilla Chips. Set in a Mexican cantina, two musicians are singing a ballad in Spanish (Figure 2). A very British voice provides the translation of a story about a woman who made her fortune from selling tortilla chips, only for it to be discovered that she imported them from Medomsley Road, Consett, County Durham. Closed down by the ministry of 'cruel but fair trading' (a Pythonesque reference), she now lives in abject poverty. There are several jokes included in the story, from the man with the laughably small moustache to the customer being given a piece of cactus to eat.

The work was a significant volte-face from the previous campaign and broke all the rules of snacks advertising. First, there is no pack shot and no one is eating the product. The only reference to the brand is in the translation of the song and in the end frame, where a self-mocking voice says: 'Pay attention. Phileas Fogg authentic snacks, made in Medomsley Road, Consett.' Second, having spent five years claiming authenticity for the products, the ad was making a feature out of the fact that the products were made in a blighted steel town in the North of England. Not surprisingly, some people were nervous about the idea. But supporters within the agency and at the client felt that the Consett location had a humour and honesty that was entirely appropriate to the brand. In its 'go for it' style, Derwent Valley decided not to test the ad and it first appeared on TV in May 1988. Predictably, it divided people. For some it was meaningless, but to others it was both exciting and entertaining. Most importantly, it helped to define the brand's personality and create an emotional link with the consumer.

The second and third ads in the series extended the humour. In 'Colonial' a veteran colonialist talks in Japanese to the audience, while having tea. He recounts his story of searching the Punjab for Punjab Puri snacks, while being supported by money from a relative in Chelmsford (another Pythonesque quirk). In his quest he has lost his son, his wife and 5,000 sherpas — and, of course, he could have found Punjab Puri in Medomsley Road, Consett. Although the character is plainly British, the voice-over tells us that after his adventure he became Japanese. Although this ad does contain a pack shot of Punjab Puri, the irreverence of the first execution remains. In the final ad, 'Jean Basteaux' (Figure 3), the humour gets even more bizarre, but it does contain one marvellous line. After hearing that Jean Basteaux was once the most famous crouton chef in France, until Phileas Fogg Mignons Morceaux came along and ruined him, we are told that 'Now he, too, is just another crouton floating on the bouillabaisse of life.'

HOT AND COOL

Following the success of the Medomsley Road branding, Derwent Valley developed two new Tortilla Chip variants: extra hot, and cool — a variety flavoured with sour cream and aromatic herbs. It

sound; location effects and music to end
male; THE MEN OF THE DESERT LEGION

DESPERATE MEN

RUINED MEN

MEN WHO HAVE SOMETHING TO FORGET

ONE SUCH PITIABLE CASE
IS JEAN BASTEAUX

ONCE THE FINEST GARLIC CROUTON
CHEF IN ALL OF FRANCE

HIS CREATIONS THE ENVY OF PARIS

THE JE NE SAIS QUOI
LE WEEKEND

LA BOHEME

LE CUL DE SAC

LE BLOB

......

Figure 3 The Bouillabaisse of Life

......

SEVEN TIMES WINNER

OF THE COVETED
CROUTON D'OR

UNTIL AT THE HEIGHT OF HIS FAME
FROM MEDOMSLEY ROAD CONSETT
COUNTY DURHAM CAME

MIGNON MORCEAUX

GARLIC CROUTONS

EVERY BIT AS GOOD

NOW HE TOO

IS JUST ANOTHER CROUTON

FLOATING ON THE
BOUILLABAISSE OF LIFE

2nd male; PAY ATTENTION PHILEAS FOGG
AUTHENTIC SNACKS

MADE IN MEDOMSLEY ROAD CONSETT.

was clear to BBH that although the humour of the previous advertising should be continued, the difference in taste delivery had to be clearly signalled. The initial thought was to produce two separate ads for cool and extra hot, but it became clear as ideas were developed that the only way to get across the cool was in contrast to the hot.

The first TV execution features two girls in a cinema, who see a boy in front of them. One of the girls says, 'Here, Tracy, it's that Tony, you used to fancy him.' The other says, 'Not any more, he smokes!' We then see the boy pouring smoke out of his collar as he eats a bag of extra hot Tortilla Chips. As he is evicted, the cinema announcer reminds the patrons that smoking is not permitted in the cinema, by order of the Chief Fire Officer, Medomsley Road, Consett. A version of the TV execution was also produced as a poster, which mimicked the advertising of a well-known cigarette brand (Figure 4).

The second TV ad in the series (Figure 5), seemingly starts as a corporate ad on the importance of the conservation of water. However, just as we are taken in by the imagery, we see a tap pouring water into the mouth of a rotund, red-faced man in polka dot shorts, who has just been eating extra hot chips. The message is that in order to save water you should stick to cool Tortilla Chips. Both ads are effective in stressing the product attributes and Cool Tortilla is expected to achieve sales of £1million in its first year to October 1992.

THE RESULTS

Derwent Valley continue to develop new products and have just launched a Pakora snack with some irreverent advertising. The rate of product innovation, coupled with the advertising support, has been key to the development of a new brand against considerable odds. Phil Adams of BBH says:

> Innovation is what keeps Phileas Fogg apart from own label. It positions us as being more interesting than the competition. And what our advertising does is create the feeling of innovation, both of product and in the way you communicate with people.

The ads seemed to have worked on many levels. The development

Figure 4 Mimicking cigarette advertising

Figure 5 Stressing product attributes

of a distinctive brand personality has helped sales to jump significantly from 1988 onwards (figure 6). Awareness of the brand has increased and now stands at 84 per cent among a London ABC1 audience. Advertising awareness has increased and reached 65 per cent among ABC1, 16 – 39 year olds, after the three Medomsley Road ads were first shown on TV. Market research has also shown that 80 per cent of buyers rate the brand as expensive, but worth it. Although we are in recessionary times and sophisticated snacks might seem a luxury, Phileas Fogg seems to have all the attributes necessary to survive and prosper. It may have had some product failures (as well as successes) along the way, but it has been consistently willing to take risks, both with product innovation and with its advertising.

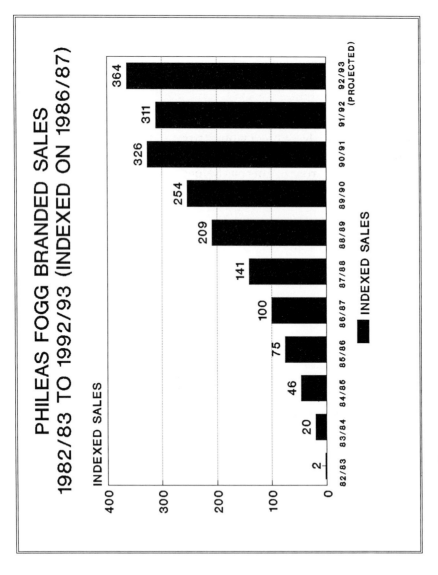

Figure 6 Phileas Fogg branded sales 1982/83 to 1992/93

Points to Note

- Phileas Fogg is an example of a brand which was launched into an under-exploited market niche and then exploited wholeheartedly. Everything about the brand, from price to packaging to distribution, sent out a clear quality message.

- Phileas Fogg set out to challenge the norms of the industry by developing a brand rather than a series of products.

- The tone of the advertising has been consistently self-mocking and irreverent. This has not only been appropriate to the target market, but also reflective of Derwent Valley's corporate culture.

- Derwent Valley have been willing to take well-informed risks and have not been frightened of changing the advertising approach. This has helped to ensure that the advertising has continued to be relevant.

- The advertising has helped to create an highly distinctive brand personality, which is always noticed and is highly popular with some consumers. That it doesn't work for everyone has never led agency or client to compromise.

References

[1] 'Australia: Phileas Fogg foods breaking into local market', *Business Review Weekly*, 6 March 1992, p79.
[2] 'Company Profile — Derwent Valley Foods', *Supermarketing*, 3 April 1992, p38

14

APPLE COMPUTERS

THE EUROPEAN LAUNCH OF THE MACINTOSH POWERBOOK

IT'S NOT A COMPUTER YOU NEED, IT'S A MACINTOSH POWERBOOK

Whereas some of the advertising campaigns in this book became international unintentionally (Absolut, Gold Blend, Nike), the European launch of the Macintosh Powerbook — Apple's version of the laptop computer — was conceived as an international campaign from the start. Although some of Apple's earlier work, such as the famous *1984* advertisement directed by Ridley Scott, was shown internationally, the Powerbook was the company's first attempt at a co-ordinated launch. Not surprisingly, the process of implementation was fraught with difficulty, not least because Apple operates a multi-local structure, where individual country managers enjoy much autonomy. This provides them with the opportunity to react to local market conditions, but it makes centralisation of such things as advertising, anathema. In spite of these difficulties, the Powerbook launch was hugely successful. Within three months of launch, it achieved a 25 per cent share of the European market for portable computers; a success that can be attributed to an outstanding product, strong advertising and — importantly in a market which is increasingly dominated by price — a genuine set of distinctive and relevant brand values.

APPLE AS A BRAND

Since its early days in the 1970s, Apple has achieved success by standing apart from other computer manufacturers. It hasn't followed the competition; rather, it has pursued its own idio-syncratic and innovative course, based on easy-to-use computers and software. The launch of the Macintosh and the *1984* ad were typical of Apple's humanistic view of a world where people, and how they think and act, is the motivating force. In contrast, IBM's credo is corporatist rather than personal — the Big Brother of computers. Reading US advertising agency Chiat/Day's description of the creative development of *1984*, one can sense the almost missionary-like zeal of Apple:

> The ad [*1984*] argues that computers will add another element of democratisation to society. Rather than having some big computer in a basement somewhere which only a few people would have access to, Apple's hope was to take that power and put it on the desk of every individual, giving everyone the same access to information.[1]

There is none of the arcane language so favoured by the competition. Apple advertising, like the product, is designed to be accessible. Indeed, print advertising produced in the early 1980s by Chiat/Day stressed the difference between Apple and its rivals in these terms:

> Of the 235 million people in America, only a fraction can use a computer. Introducing Macintosh. For the rest of us.

This empowering approach was also being adopted in Europe. Apple's French agency, CLM/BBDO, produced a TV commercial which communicated Apple's values by drawing a comparison between Apple/other computers and the telegraph/telephone. The film, known as *Morse*, starts with rows of people in nineteenth century costumes learning the rigours of the morse code. Their practice session is interrupted by the news that Alexander Graham Bell has invented the telephone. The ad cuts to rows of people in white coats learning the codes necessary to use personal computers. In turn, their practice session is interrupted by the news that Apple has invented the Macintosh. The inference is that the Macintosh will change the way we think about computers in just the same way as the invention of the telephone changed the way we think about communications. The ad does not attempt to sell the features of the Macintosh — that more detailed role is normally the task of the press — but it does endorse Apple's distinctive personality.

CLM/BBDO recognise that, periodically, the Apple culture needs to be restated. It is partly this that keeps Apple from being cloned in the way that IBM has been by Far Eastern competitors. Having stated the case with *Morse*, in 1990 Apple went back on TV with an execution known as *Heir*. Again, it presented Apple's culture, but in this instance there was not a computer in sight. Predictably, people were divided on its merits: critics saw it as extravagance; supporters saw it as inspired. It is the sort of split in opinion that Apple seems prepared to accept. It's fine that some people are Apple devotees and others are not, as long as everyone recognises what the company and its products stand for. The ad (Figure 1), shows an old-fashioned company being presented by a father to his son, who will one day inherit it. The father's view of managing people is autocratic: ' All these people who will be working for you are there to execute tasks and not there to think.' But there is, of course, another way of running a business, as the end frame suggests. Although unstated, the Apple way is the opposite of what we have seen: helping people to achieve their own potential. Peter Gilson, Management Supervisor at CLM/BBDO says:

> Apple's mission is to change the way you work, learn, think and communicate. To do that we've got to motivate people to augment their productivity and creativity. You'll find that in the tone of voice in all our advertising.

THE STRATEGY FOR POWERBOOK

Although Apple has a powerful set of brand values, this can in no sense compensate for a poor product. Apple's first attempt at marketing a portable computer in the late eighties was a failure. Not only was it overpriced, it was also only just portable. The Apple Macintosh Powerbook, in contrast, was small, light and very competitively priced. However, the previous failure left Apple some three years behind the competition. By the time Apple launched the Powerbook in October 1991, there were approximately 110 laptops on the market. In spite of this, Apple set the objective of achieving a 25 per cent share of the European portable market and a 15 per cent share in the long term. To put this in perspective, Apple's share of the European PC market was approximately 7 per cent. David Roman, Apple's European Director of Marketing Services, explains:

> The internal code name for the Powerbook launch in Europe was *Project 25%*, reflecting the market share goal for the

Figure 1 The Heir

A big black limousine is driving through an industrial estate.

In the back of the car sits the owner and his son. The father says 'One day all this will be yours . . . the factories, the machines, the people.'

His son sits impassively.

The father continues: 'But always remember that when it comes to making decisions you'll be all alone. You won't be able to depend on them. Their interest is not the same as yours. All these people who will be working for you are there to execute tasks and not to think.

   If they ever started to think, they would want to start changing things. And that is not within their ability. Never forget that they owe you everything.'

   Voiceover: There are various ways of running a business and this is one of them. Luckily there are others. Apple logo.

product within the first 100 days. In order to gain a leadership position, we knew we had to take a 'leadership attitude', positioning the product as more than just another notebook computer.

However, not only did the share target seem optimistic, there were also a number of barriers to success:

- Apple had never tried to launch a product on a pan-European basis before, and the multi-local organisational structure was unlikely to be conducive to achieving this.
- The previous experience with the Apple Portable created a degree of scepticism among the trade.
- Distribution channels were primarily limited to Apple dealerships.
- It was unlikely that advertising budgets would enable Apple to outspend the competition.

To counter these negatives, the single most important factor — outside the product itself — was the value conferred by the Apple brand, which had been built up over time with the help of such campaigns as *Morse* and *Heir*. This not only gave Apple a head start with the Powerbook, but because the ideology campaigns had not dwelt on computer specifics, there was an awareness and image of Apple among non-users of computers. If Apple was going to achieve its targeted 25 per cent share, it had to reach into this larger target market of non-users, as well as the already committed. The task of converting non-users was nothing new to Apple. Indeed, it had been the guiding principle of the company since its formation:

> In naming his new company Apple, Steve Jobs demystified computers and computing. He recognised that the future of his new business lay not with the fanatical, knowledgeable computer expert, but with the man and woman in the street. He had to appeal to an audience which knew nothing about computers and did not wish to know anything.[2]

From research, CLM/BBDO concluded that the reason non-users had not yet entered the market was because all the current offerings presented themselves either as 'hyped up calculators' or as technologically complex computers. Not only did these consumers find the idea of having to learn about computers frightening, but because computer manufacturers were not consumer-oriented in their communications, they did not perceive the need to have one. To get the non-users over the personal computer barrier, Apple had to position the Powerbook as different from anything else on the market. Consumers had to believe that the Powerbook could do things for them which were above and beyond what they thought computers could do. This determined a strategic focus on what the Powerbook does, rather than what it is — a focus that was likely to work all the harder for being in tune with Apple's consumer-led brand image.

In just the same way as Sony had branded the Walkman as a distinctive category rather than as a portable cassette player, so the Apple Macintosh Powerbook would have an identity in its own right. If it was going to distance itself from the competition and overcome the negatives that had been created in the minds of non-users, words such as 'Laptop' and 'Notebook' would have to be taboo. The new strategy would be built out of the strategic line: 'It's not a computer you need, it's a Macintosh Powerbook.' CLM/BBDO's concluding thought in their recommendation was:

> We believe that we can pull the Macintosh Powerbook away from the laptop product category, and sell many more than with it staying clearly in there.

DEVELOPING THE CREATIVE WORK

BBDO presented the above strategy informally to Apple in July 1991. It was agreed by senior management and the agency went to work on the development of a creative brief. As the work was going to run in 16 countries, it was decided that a number of BBDO offices should also be involved in the creative development. The Germans, British, French, Danes, Swedes and Americans all developed ideas for a print campaign that were vetted internally by BBDO. For the presentation of the work to the client, it was decided that all the campaigns would be submitted to the sixteen country managers, but the origin of each campaign would not be stated. The idea of presenting six campaigns to sixteen countries may seem akin to trying to reach agreement on GATT, but there was almost unanimous support for the French work. It not only seemed to be strategically correct, it was clearly part of the Apple heritage.

The French campaign was built on the idea that non-users see a computer as a machine for typing letters, crunching numbers and sorting through databases. However, the way most people think is randomly rather than in numbers. What a Powerbook could do is provide somewhere to put random thoughts and moments of inspiration. The French creative team came up with the idea of overcoming preconceptions about computers by showing a ripped tablecloth corner with various ideas sketched on it. The copy would simply say, 'Ideas come suddenly. That's to say anywhere, anyhow. It's not a computer you need. It's a Macintosh Power-book.' In other words, the Powerbook is for storing ideas, not data.

However good the concept seemed, it didn't work as a European campaign. Most countries simply didn't use paper tablecloths. Also, the concept didn't show what the Powerbook would look like, as this was foreseen as a later stage of the campaign. Nevertheless, it was decided to try to introduce the concept and show the Powerbook in one hit. Consequently, the campaign changed in two ways. First, the tablecloth idea was expanded to include other devices on which people might scribble impromptu ideas. These included metro tickets, matchbooks, hands, beer mats and newspapers. Second, an additional sequential page was added to the tablecloth showing a closed Powerbook. Although the copy made certain claims for the product, it was felt to be important that people couldn't see what the product actually looked like and perhaps dismiss it as just another laptop computer.

With the changes, there seemed to be unanimous agreement on the creative approach. However, because of the multi-local structure of Apple, it was felt that each country should produce its own ads, rather than centralising the process. This would make the achievement of uniformity more difficult, but it was more appropriate to Apple's culture and structure. Within this con-straint, CLM/BBDO tried to keep the implementation as tight as possible by providing a set of written guidelines to all sixteen countries on how the ads should be constructed. Then as each office produced its interpretation of the idea, their work was called back into Paris for review. The resultant ads have a fair degree of uniformity, although there are some rogues. The Dutch advertising features a copy line borrowed from the American

Les idées vous viennent brusquement,
c'est-à-dire n'importe où, n'importe comment.

Continuez de travailler à votre manière.

Ce n'est pas d'un ordinateur dont vous avez besoin, c'est d'un Macintosh PowerBook.   Apple

Macintosh PowerBook.   Apple

Figure 2   French and German advertisements compared

Weshalb Sie ein PowerBook brauchen und keinen Computer.

Das PowerBook von Apple.

Apple

Geistesblitze kommen zu den ungelegensten Gelegenheiten.
Deshalb brauchen Sie keinen Computer, sondern eine neue Idee.

Nächsten Montag sind Sie auf alles vorbereitet.

Apple

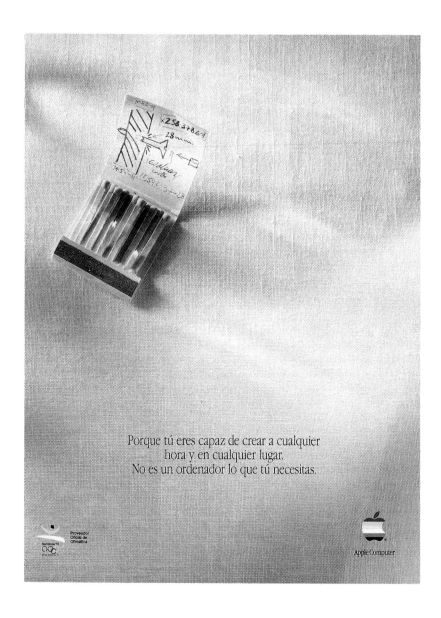

Figure 3 Ideological page from Spain

campaign that was presented to the committee: 'Macintosh Powerbook. It's the next thing.' Similarly, the British version of the tablecloth concentrates on a stylish shot of a dinner table, complete with Mont Blanc pen — missing the point that the creative idea is the tabletop scribbling, not the setting. Nonetheless when, for example, the French version of tablecloth is set side by side with the German beer mat (figure 2), the similarities are evident. Peter Gilson says:

> Apple wanted the countries to be able to adapt the work. And when you look across the whole range of ads, it's quite uniform, especially for a campaign done multi-locally. There's a continuity of tone and there's a continuity of message and there's a continuity of visual concept.

THE LAUNCH

Once all the ads had been developed and reviewed by the centre, everything was geared towards the co-ordinated European launch on 17 October 1991. The media was primarily black-and-white national and regional press, although the allocation of money and choice of publications was determined by the countries, not by any centralised team. The campaign had an almost immediate impact, in spite of the fact that the hoped for increase in the number of outlets selling the product did not materialise. There was certainly a lot of pent-up demand from Apple devotees, which fuelled initial sales, but as the communication began to reach the non-users, sales accelerated. The feedback which BBDO got from the markets suggested that it was the ideological positioning page (figure 3) which was intriguing people. Peter Gilson believes it was the 'uncomputer'-like feel of the ads that made the impact:

> We got through to those people who had not really considered computers before, because the advertising was simple to understand. It was clean and new and not how computers are normally advertised. The product itself was great and the advertising was good enough to break through the clutter.

The result: Apple achieved, against the odds, a 25 per cent share of the European portable computer market within 100 days of launch, making a significant contribution to Apple's earnings in the period. Only time will tell whether the 15 per cent long term market share is achievable.

Points to Note

- Apple is an example of a planned European advertising campaign which had to overcome the limitations of a multi-local structure, where countries enjoy considerable autonomy.

- Although the Powerbook was launched in a highly competitive market, Apple enjoyed the advantage conferred by strongly branded advertising over a number of years.

- The advertising campaign for Powerbook was supportive of the Apple culture and enabled the company to target the large market of non-users.

- The creative approach was built on the way people think, rather than the functional performance of the product. It also provided Apple with the opportunity of distancing the Powerbook from other laptops.

References

[1] *Chiat/Day: The First Twenty Years*, Rizzoli, New York, 1990

[2] *Brands: An International Review by Interbrand*, Mercury Business Books, 1990

FURTHER READING

Chernotony de, Leslie and McDonald, Malcolm, *Creating Powerful Brands*, Butterworth-Heinemann, Oxford, 1992.

Cowley, Don. (ed), *Understanding Brands*, Kogan Page, London, 1991

Interbrand, *Brands: An International Review by Interbrand*, Mercury Business Books, London, 1990

Jones, John Philip, *What's in a Name? Advertising and the Concept of Brands*, Lexington Books, Lexington, Massachusetts, 1986

Jones, John Philip, *Does it pay to Advertise?*, Lexington Books, Lexington, Massachusetts, 1989

King, Stephen, *Developing New Brands*, JWT, London, 1984

McDonald, Malcom and Cavusgil, S Tamer, *The International Marketing Digest*, Heinemann, Oxford, 1990

Ogilvy, David, *Ogilvy on Advertising*, Crown Books, New York, 1983

Strasser, J B and Becklund, L, *The Story of Nike and the Men Who Played There*, Harcourt Brace Jovanovich, New York, 1991

INDEX